MASTER EUROPEAN PAINTINGS

MASTER EUROPEAN PAINTINGS

FROM THE NATIONAL GALLERY OF IRELAND

•

MANTEGNA TO GOYA

THE NATIONAL GALLERY
OF IRELAND
1992

This catalogue was published in connection with the exhibition
'Master European Paintings from The National Gallery of Ireland : Mantegna to Goya':

The Art Institute of Chicago from 6 June to 9 August 1992,
The Fine Arts Museums of San Francisco from 19 September to 6 December 1992,
The Museum of Fine Arts, Boston from 13 January to 28 March 1993,
The IBM Gallery of Science and Art, New York from 27 April to 26 June 1993.

This touring exhibition was made possible by the IBM Corporation.

It has been organised by The National Gallery of Ireland
in cooperation with The Art Institute of Chicago.

An indemnity was provided by the Federal Council on the Arts and the Humanities.
Transatlantic shipment was provided courtesy of Aer Lingus.
The assistance of the Irish American Cultural Institute is acknowledged.

British Library Cataloguing-in-Publication Data
Keaveney, Raymond et al.
Master European Paintings from The National Gallery of Ireland : Mantegna to Goya.
I. Title
708.291835

ISBN 0903162636 Pbk
ISBN 0903162644 Hb

Published by The National Gallery of Ireland
Edited by Helen Litton
Designed and Produced by Creative Inputs
Colour Reproduction and Printing by Nicholson & Bass

Front cover *detail* — *Julie Bonaparte as Queen of Spain with her Daughters, Zénaïde and Charlotte.*
Baron François~Pascal~Simon Gérard (1770-1837).

Page 2 *detail* — *The Castle of Bentheim.*
Jacob van Ruisdael (1628/9-1682).

Page 6 *detail* — *Allegory of the Immaculate Conception.*
Giovanni Battista Tiepolo (1696-1770).

Page 25 *detail* — *Thomas Conolly.*
Anton Raphael Mengs (1728-1779).

End Papers *detail* — *Queen Victoria and Prince Albert Opening the 1853 Dublin Great Exhibition.*
James Mahoney (1810-1879).

CONTENTS

INTRODUCTION

Virtually from its inauguration in 1864, the National Gallery of Ireland has sent paintings abroad on exhibition, in a spirit of sharing its treasures with cultural institutions elsewhere. Traditionally this has involved the loan of individual works to shows dedicated to a particular artist or theme. Rarely have overseas audiences had an opportunity to appreciate, at a single showing, the range of the collection which, since its establishment in 1854, has grown to include over two and a half thousand works representing all the major schools and periods of European art.

With home audiences now reaching over one million visitors per annum, it has become necessary to effect substantial improvements to the elegant, but much worn, fabric of the Gallery, as well as planning a new wing to accommodate additional facilities. This comprehensive programme has prompted the initiative of sending some of the Gallery's most precious masterpieces abroad whilst work is in progress. That this project has come to fruition is largely due to the support of IBM, who early on recognised the unique opportunity which these circumstances presented. The Governors and Guardians of the National Gallery of Ireland are most grateful to Mr. John Akers and the Board of the IBM Corporation for their generous sponsorship. Further progress with the exhibition was achieved with the agreement of the Art Institute of Chicago to undertake the local administration of the show. The Gallery Board wish to thank Mr. James Wood, Director, The Art Institute of Chicago, Mr. Harry S. Parker III, Director, The Fine Arts Museums of San Francisco, and Mr. Alan Shestack, Director, The Museum of Fine Arts, Boston, and their colleagues, for the warm and enthusiastic support received from their institutions in promoting the event. A special note of thanks must also be extended to Mr. Richard Berglund at the IBM Gallery of Science and Art in New York, which will be the final venue for the show. We are grateful for the helpful assistance and co-operation of Mr. Dermot Gallagher, the Irish Ambassador to the United States of America, to the staff of the Embassy and of the Consulates in Chicago, San Francisco, Boston and New York.

As this exhibition represents the most significant presentation of Ireland's National Collection to an American audience, we are particularly grateful to have received the support of the Federal Council on the Arts and the Humanities, who have provided an indemnity for the exhibits. The support of the Irish American Cultural Institute is also acknowledged, as is the assistance of Aer Lingus, who have provided transportation for the paintings.

Raymond Keaveney
Director, National Gallery of Ireland.

ACKNOWLEDGEMENTS

The National Gallery of Ireland wishes to acknowledge the assistance of the following people:

The IBM Corporation - John Akers, John Cunningham, Dolores Gostkowski.

The IBM Gallery of Science and Art - Richard Berglund, Robert Murdock.

IBM Ireland - William Burgess, Pauline Knight.

The Art Institute of Chicago - James Wood, Robert Mars, Dorothy Schroeder, Martha Wolff, Larry Feinberg, Mary Solt, Mary Mulhern, Mary Jane Keitel, Marija Raudys, Bill Leisher, Faye Wrubel, Tom Veach, Eileen Harakal, Ted Spiegel, Larry Ter Molen.

The Fine Arts Museums of San Francisco - Harry Parker, Stephen Nash, Lynn Orr, Marion Stewart, Debra Pughe.

The Museum of Fine Arts, Boston - Alan Shestack, Peter Sutton, Eric Zafran, Desirée Caldwell, Catherine King, Linda Thomas.

Aer Lingus - Cathal Mullan, Brian Scanlon, Eddie Kelly.

The Irish American Cultural Institute - John Walsh, Michelle Lynch.

Creative Inputs - Michael Breen, Terry Monaghan.

Nicholson & Bass - Robert South, Henry Ballentine.

FOREWORD

Ireland has a special place in the history and culture of most of America's older cities. Her history and literature are well known to many Americans, but the extraordinary collections of her National Gallery have been experienced by relatively few on this side of the Atlantic. This beautiful exhibition of *Master European Paintings from the National Gallery of Ireland* is therefore doubly welcome as both a remarkable survey of Old Master European painting and as a means for our American audience to understand more fully the rich culture of Dublin.

The National Gallery of Ireland has only once before lent a group of works of this quality, size, and scope to another institution, when, in 1985, a selection of masterpiece paintings travelled to the National Gallery in London. Since the time of that exhibition, the Irish Gallery's collection has continued to grow impressively, through purchases and the generous gifts of numerous donors. We are very grateful that several of the most important of these recent acquisitions have been included in this exhibition, among them outstanding paintings by Velázquez, Hobbema, and Ruisdael. Of course, one of the great benefits of an exhibition such as this, is that it provides the opportunity for the participating museums to display works by masters not represented in their own collections. The dazzling array of seventeenth-century paintings in the exhibition includes important works by Le Nain, Duyster and Drost, artists whose paintings are found in few American museums. This exhibition also allows the host institutions to 'expand' their own holdings, to understand better the paintings in their own collection by comparing them to borrowed works by the same artists. In this respect, perhaps the most interesting and delightful opportunity that this exhibition offers is the chance to reunite, at the first venue, Conrad Faber's portrait of *Katherina Knoblauch*, one of the exquisite sixteenth-century German paintings in Ireland's collection, with Faber's companion portrait of her husband, Friedrich Rohrbach, in the Art Institute of Chicago.

It is with great appreciation that we welcome this loan of forty-four of the National Gallery's most precious treasures. And it is our hope that this exhibition, made possible by the generous support of the IBM Corporation, will be only the first of many cooperative projects undertaken by the National Gallery of Ireland and America's museums.

James N. Wood
Director, The Art Institute of Chicago

Harry S. Parker III
Director, The Fine Arts Museums of San Francisco

Alan Shestack
Director, Museum of Fine Arts, Boston

Fig. 1 *The National Gallery of Ireland, main entrance. To the left is the original 1864 wing; the Milltown wing, opened in 1903, is in the centre and to the right is the 1968 extension*

THE TASTE FOR OLD MASTERS

The Act of Parliament establishing the National Gallery of Ireland in August 1854 reflects contemporary admiration and appreciation for the works of the old masters. It also reflects the aspiration of nineteenth-century society to emulate the achievements of the preceding centuries by providing young artists with a readily accessible range of models of excellence as aids to their education. The general public were also to benefit from the establishment of a National Gallery, as the institution was to be accessible to all without charge.

The taste for old master paintings came to maturity in Ireland in the mid-eighteenth century, at a time when many of the most distinguished members of the local aristocracy travelled to Europe on the Grand Tour to finish their education and collect objects of *vertu* for their town and country residences. In respect of the formation of the Gallery collection, the most notable of these travellers was Joseph Leeson (1711-1783), subsequently to become the 1st Earl of Milltown. A member of a prosperous Dublin family which had made its fortune from brewing and banking, he made his first visit to Italy in 1744, where he not only had the opportunity to educate himself on that country's distinguished tradition in the arts, but also had the good fortune to gain the services of Pompeo Batoni to paint his portrait (see Cat. no. 2). He must also have spent considerable time looking for works of art to decorate his new country mansion at Russborough in County Wicklow, then being constructed to the designs of the German architect Richard Castle. Among his most notable acquisitions are the set of four Roman *Capricci* by Giovanni Paolo Panini (NGI Inv. no. 725-28). Later, almost all of the paintings which he and his descendants purchased on this and subsequent visits to Italy, or had acquired elsewhere, including Poussin's *Holy Family with St. Anne, St. Elizabeth and the Young St. John* (see Cat. no. 28), were to enter the National Gallery as part of the gift made by Geraldine, widow of the 6th and last Earl of Milltown, in 1902.

The pretensions of the British and Irish 'Grand Tourists' are satirised in a parody of Raphael's great fresco *The School of Athens* (fig. 2), which was painted in Rome in 1751 by Sir Joshua Reynolds. This mock-heroic composition, by the future president of the Royal Academy, swarms with caricatures of some of the most notable British and Irish personalities who were in Rome at this time. Besides Joseph Leeson, who is the figure to the left standing under the gothic arch, it includes the figure of Lord Charlemont, who plays the recorder in the musical trio placed in the foreground, and Joseph Henry of Straffan, the nephew of Joseph Leeson, shown reclining on the steps in imitation of the pose of Diogenes in Raphael's fresco. Charlemont, known as the Volunteer Earl, one of the most influential figures in Irish society of the time, spent nine years on the Grand Tour, including trips to Egypt and Greece, where he was among the first to take an interest in the antiquities of the area. In Rome he became friendly with Piranesi, whose *Antichità Romane* was originally dedicated to him. On his return to Ireland he employed Sir William Chambers to design his new town house in Rutland Square (now home to Dublin's Hugh Lane Municipal Gallery), and his Casino at Marino, on the outskirts of the city, a building designed according to the

Fig. 2 *Joshua Reynolds (1723-92),* A Parody on Raphael's School of Athens (1751). *Milltown Gift, 1902. (NGI Inv. no. 734)*

principles of the finest Italian models. Yet for all the time he spent in Italy, his taste was not exclusively confined to classical art or Italian art, and Rembrandt's *Judas Returning the Thirty Pieces of Silver* (private collection, England) formed part of his superb collection. Joseph Henry, who almost certainly commissioned the caricature from Reynolds, spent virtually as many years abroad as Charlemont. His residence at Straffan in County Kildare housed a fine collection of pictures, including views of the Roman Campagna which he had commissioned from Richard Wilson (NGI Inv. nos. 746 and 747) and Strozzi's allegorical piece, *Spring and Summer* (see Cat. no. 36) which had been acquired by the family in 1856 from Signor Aducci in Rome (who was later to supply paintings to the newly-founded gallery).

Further evidence of the growing taste for old master paintings can be found in written accounts describing the contents of the homes of the landed gentry and professional classes, of which there were a great many. Mark Bence-Jones has listed almost two thousand such buildings in his published survey of Irish country houses and many of these would have been decorated with the works of the great masters or their followers. Owners who took particular pride in their collections went as far as having them published in specially compiled volumes. In 1856 Adam Macrory, one of the Belfast firm of solicitors Macrory Sons and Boyd, published his collection of eighty-five paintings which hung at his home in Duncairn, listing among the works to be found there a number of pictures attributed to Schalcken, Titian and Annibale Carracci. In the published record of his collection at Castle Bernard in County Cork,

Fig. 3 *Anton Raphael Mengs (1728-79),* A Seated Male Nude. *Black chalk with white highlights on paper. (NGI Inv. no. 3930)*

the Earl of Bandon in 1866 listed one hundred and twenty pictures, including compositions attributed to Titian, Dürer and David Teniers. Auction records which survive from the nineteenth century list countless works by the continental masters, many of which are given attributions which would not stand up to modern scrutiny. That said, the optimistic attributions are in themselves indicative of the thriving trade in old master pictures, and undoubtedly there were many genuine masterpieces among the vast number of second-rate works put on the market.

An appreciation of the works of the great masters and an understanding of their working procedures were soon perceived to be essential elements in the education of young local artists, especially if they were ever to aspire to supplying their well-travelled patrons with new works. With no proper academies established and few collections available for inspection, students were forced to consider the need to travel abroad to complete their training. One of the first to do so was James Latham, who journeyed to Antwerp in 1724. Whilst there, he attended life classes and other forms of instruction not then available in Dublin, and he had the opportunity to admire the achievements of the local school in the many public buildings and private collections he would have visited. This lack of facilities at home was partly made up for in 1740 by the establishment of the Dublin Society Schools, where students were provided with tuition in the elements of drawing and design. To assist with their instruction a small collection of drawings and academic studies was acquired, including examples of the work of Watteau, Claude Vignon and Anton Raphael Mengs (fig. 3). Yet such was the new-found enthusiasm for the art of the continental masters that many talented young painters and sculptors were advised by their patrons to spend some time away, particularly in Italy. In the latter part of the eighteenth century

Fig. 4 *James Mahoney (1810-79),* The Fourth Visit by Queen Victoria and Prince Albert to the 1853 Dublin Great Exhibition. *Watercolour on paper. (NGI Inv. no. 2452)*

Dublin's 'Crystal Palace' *was designed by the Sligo-born architect, John Benson. It covered 6 1/2 acres in total and the Great Hall, shown in Mahoney's watercolour, was 425 feet long, 100 feet wide and 105 feet high.*

many Irish artists travelled to the continent to finish their training. Among the most distinguished members of this group were James Barry (1741-1806) and Hugh Douglas Hamilton (c. 1739-1808). Barry spent some five years on the continent, studying mostly in Rome, where he acquired a taste for history painting in the grand manner. The effects of his Italian sojourn (1766-1771) can be noted in one of the compositions which he executed whilst in Rome, *The Temptation of Adam and Eve* (1770, NGI Inv. no. 762), in which he attempts to emulate the monumental and idealised figure style of the great masters. His most ambitious essay in this pursuit was his cycle of decorations for the great Room of the Society of Arts, in the Adelphi in London, where he painted six large scenes representing *The Progress of Human Culture* (1776-1783). Prior to his departure for Italy, Hugh Douglas Hamilton concentrated almost exclusively on a small scale, drawing portraits in pastel. Like Barry, his sojourn in Italy, where he lived for almost thirteen years (1779-1792), transformed his style and gave him the confidence to work in oil and on a much larger scale, producing life-size portraits and subject pictures. Whilst in Rome he formed a friendship with the sculptor Antonio Canova, whose work may have provided the inspiration for the canvas painting, *Cupid and Psyche* (c.1793), which he painted soon after his return home to Dublin.

It is not surprising that the idea of establishing a public picture gallery in Dublin soon took root. Indeed, the first serious consideration given to the establishment of such a gallery goes back to the eighteenth century when the Society of Artists, founded in 1764, considered the notion of adding a permanent picture gallery to their premises in William Street. Under the Viceroyalty of the Duke of Rutland, more definite plans were drawn up for the formation of a National Gallery, with the Flemish artist Peter De Gree being appointed as its first Keeper. The project collapsed, unfortunately, following the death of the Duke in 1787. Quite coincidentally, the elegant fountain erected to his memory in 1791 by his many admirers stands today directly opposite the entrance to the Gallery on Merrion Square. No further initiative of any consequence occurred until 1853, when the Irish Industrial Exhibition took place in Dublin.

This extraordinary event, modelled on the Great Exhibition in London in 1851, was held in the grounds of the Dublin Society's property on Leinster Lawn, in the heart of the capital. Underwritten by William Dargan, the most important railway magnate of his day and architect of the world's first commuter rail link from Dublin to Dun Laoghaire, the event was housed in a series of glazed pavilions (fig. 4) which, over the period from May to October of that year, drew a total attendance of 1,149,369 visitors. A major attraction of the exhibition was the Fine Arts Hall which featured a collection of over one thousand pictures, including a substantial collection of old master pictures made available from local collections, such as those of the Earl of Milltown and the Earl of Charlemont. Indeed, such was the success of this element of the exhibition that on its closure a new body, The Irish Institution, was formed for the purpose of holding further exhibitions and with the ultimate aim of establishing a National Gallery. This body seized the opportunity to achieve its ambition by uniting with the Dargan Committee, a group formed to honour the magnanimity of the promoter of the Irish Industrial Exhibition. Less than one year later, in August 1854,

Fig. 5 *Ferdinand Bol (1616-80),* David's Dying Charge to Solomon. *(1643, NGI Inv. no. 47)*

an Act of Parliament was passed 'to provide for the establishment of a National Gallery of Paintings...'

It took ten years to fund, design and construct the gallery building, during which time the newly-appointed Board of Governors and Guardians enthusiastically set about forming the collection through the solicitation of gifts and by way of purchases made with the modest funds at their disposal. The first significant painting to enter the collection was Ferdinand Bol's imposing canvas *David's Dying Charge to Solomon* (fig. 5) which was presented to the Gallery in 1854 by the Lord Lieutenant, the Earl of St. Germans. Over the following ten years, the Board continued to build up the collection through the addition of further purchases and gifts, of which the most significant were the sixteen paintings acquired in 1856 from the collection of Cardinal Fesch, the uncle of Napoleon, through the agency of Robert McPherson in Rome, among them Carlo Maratta's *The Rape of Europa* (NGI Inv. no. 81). A further twenty-three works were acquired from Rome in the same year, including two great canvases by Giovanni Lanfranco which had originally formed part of the artist's commission for San Paolo Fuori le Mure just outside Rome. Among the other works acquired at this time were the *Vanitas Fruit-piece* (see Cat. no. 16) by Jan Davidsz. de Heem (London, Blamire sale, Christie's, November, 1863), and Jordaens' massive *Veneration of the Eucharist* (London, 1863, fig. 6).

Fig. 6 *Jacob Jordaens (1593-1678),* The Veneration of the Eucharist *(early 1630's, NGI Inv. no. 46)*

Fig. 7 *A view from the grand staircase of the 1864 wing, National Gallery of Ireland*

The foundation stone of the new building was laid in January 1859, following much controversy over its design and cost. Originally it had been intended to allocate just £11,000 towards the construction of the gallery, which echoed the exterior design of Frederick Clarendon's newly-completed Natural History Museum, on the southern flank of Leinster Lawn. The commission to design the building first went to Charles Lanyon, but doubts concerning his plans and the construction costs (estimated at £23,000) led to his dismissal and the appointment of Francis Fowke (1823-1865) to the project. Fowke, a native of County Tyrone, was well equipped for the task; he had previously been responsible for the design of part of the recently-established South Kensington Museum (now the Victoria & Albert) in London, where he developed a range of top-lit galleries specifically for the display of pictures. In Dublin, he had the opportunity to further develop his ideas and the resultant building constituted, at the time of its completion in 1864, one of the most modern and advanced facilities of its kind at the time. It boasted a handsome suite of top-lit picture galleries which in winter time were illuminated by an array of 2,000 gas burners. To counteract the threat of fire, the floors were fireproofed through the implementation of a revolutionary construction process which employed steel and concrete, anticipating modern construction techniques of pre-stressed/reinforced concrete. The ground floor area, with its limited daylight, housed a collection of sculpture. Ironically, when completed, Fowke's building had cost £28,000, some five thousand pounds more than Lanyon's proposed gallery.

When the Gallery opened to the public in January 1864, there were just one hundred and twenty-five paintings in the collection. Today, the number has grown to more than two and a half thousand pictures, with almost five thousand watercolours and drawings and some three thousand engravings, ranging in date from the fourteenth to the twentieth centuries and covering virtually all the major schools and phases in the development of European art. Besides its extensive holdings of European paintings, the Gallery also houses a fine collection of paintings of the national school and the national portrait collection. Despite the modest resources at its disposal, the collection was developed wisely and energetically under the stewardship of its first directors, who spread a wide net in their pursuit of suitable and affordable paintings. Among the acquisitions made by George Mulvany (1862-1869), the Gallery's first director, was Georg Pencz's *Portrait of a Man* (NGI Inv. no. 1373) which he acquired in Paris in 1864. His successor, Henry Doyle, a relative of Sir Arthur Conan Doyle, managed the affairs of the Gallery from 1869 to 1892, and made many fine purchases, most notably the beautiful nocturne *Rest on the Flight into Egypt* (NGI Inv. no. 215) by Rembrandt, obtained at Christie's in London in 1883. Doyle was followed by the eminently qualified Walter Armstrong (1892-1914) who oversaw two of the most significant developments in the early life of the institution. In 1897 Geraldine, Countess of Milltown, summoned him to her family estate at Russborough in County Wicklow to inform him of her wish to donate to the Gallery virtually the entire collection of pictures then in her house, together with furniture and the library. Among the paintings were a great many works which had been acquired by the first Earl and his descendants on various trips to the continent, including a number of important canvases of the seventeenth century Florentine school by artists such as

Fig. 8 *The Children's Art Holiday at the National Gallery of Ireland is one of the many activities organised by the Education Department. (Photograph courtesy* Irish Times*)*

Lorenzo Lippi, Felice Ficherelli and Cesare Dandini. Already, before the arrival of the Milltown Collection, the Board of Governors and Guardians had campaigned for an extension to be constructed to house the new additions to the collection, a campaign which was brought to a successful conclusion in 1903 with the opening of the new extension. It is today referred to as the Milltown Wing, because it originally displayed the two hundred paintings donated by the Dowager Countess.

Sir Hugh Lane (Director, 1914-15), who succeeded Armstrong, was a gifted connoisseur with a deep interest in both the old masters and contemporary painting, forming a personal collection which included works by Titian, Sebastiano del Piombo, Degas and Renoir. There can be little doubt that had he not drowned so tragically in 1915 when travelling back to Ireland from the United States, aboard the ill-fated *Lusitania,* he would have made an even greater contribution to the development of the collection than that which he achieved in the few years during which he was associated with the Gallery. Even as it was, with the frequent gifts he made whilst alive and the bequest made following his death, the Gallery was significantly enriched, receiving works by Claude, Goya, Titian, and del Piombo among others. The most intriguing work to enter the collection as a consequence of his generosity was John Singer Sargent's *Portrait of President Woodrow Wilson* (fig. 9), a work commissioned by the Board of the Gallery after his death in accordance with his wish to support the Red Cross whose resources had been severely stretched during the Great War. Following Lane's death, Walter Strickland, the noted compiler of the standard reference work on Irish artists, fulfilled the office of director for a brief period.

In the many years since Lane's death the collection has continued to grow under the guidance of its directors, each of whom has added his personal stamp to the collection. Despite the fact that only very modest funds were available for acquisitions, the annual purchasing grant being retained at just £1,000 for the period 1866-1937, the directors used the funds shrewdly in the pursuit of suitable pictures for the collection. Robert Langton Douglas, with his deep personal interest in Italian art, purchased a number of early Italian panel pictures, including, in 1922, the *Assumption of the Magdalen* (NGI Inv. no. 841) by the rare master Silvestro dei Gherarducci for £1,000. Lucius O'Callaghan acquired Strozzi's *Spring and Summer* (see Cat. no. 36) for just £350 in 1924, whilst Thomas Bodkin obtained Lastman's *Joseph Selling Corn in Egypt* (NGI Inv. no. 890) for a modest £300 in 1927. Even more remarkable were the pictures added by George Furlong; a string of inspired purchases included Giovanni Benedetto Castiglione's *Shepherdess Spako with the Infant Cyrus* (see Cat. no. 5) which he bought in London in 1937 for £378, and even more remarkably Giuseppe Crespi's *Massacre of the Innocents* (NGI Inv. no. 1020) for just £30.

The poet and francophile, Thomas MacGreevy, had the good fortune to commence his term as Director in 1950 with the announcement of Sir Alfred Chester Beatty's gift to the nation of over ninety French paintings, among them many works by masters of the Barbizon School and by artists such as Eugène Fromentin who specialised in orientalist subjects. Also in the same year came the news that the celebrated writer and dramatist, George Bernard Shaw, had bequeathed to the Gallery a third of the residue of his estate in acknowledgement of the important part it had played in his

Fig. 9 *John Singer Sargent (1856-1925),* Woodrow Wilson *(1917, NGI Inv. no. 817)*

education as a young man when growing up in Dublin during the later years of the nineteenth century. The moneys generated from the Shaw estate, particularly after *Pygmalion* was adapted to become the phenomenally successful musical *My Fair Lady*, have ever since constituted the most important source of funds for the making of acquisitions; MacGreevy was the first to employ these funds when acquiring Domenico Tintoretto's allegorical picture, *Venice* (NGI Inv. no. 1384), in 1959. James White, who succeeded MacGreevy in 1964, oversaw the construction of the new extension which had been negotiated by his predecessor just two years prior to his retirement. Besides the addition of picture galleries, the new wing included a lecture theatre, library and restaurant, greatly enhancing the Gallery's ability to serve its public. The sixteen years of James White's stewardship witnessed a remarkable increase in visitor numbers, with attendance figures rising from 68,000 in 1964 to over 506,000 in 1977. During this time the collection continued to be built up, particularly with additions to the French school, most notably paintings by David (see Cat. no. 8), Fragonard and Vouet (see Cat. no. 41). Homan Potterton, who succeeded James White in 1980, extended the range of the collection with the addition of works by twentieth-century masters, including Chaim Soutine's *Man Walking the Stairs* (NGI Inv. no. 4485) and Emil Nolde's *Two Women in a Garden* (NGI Inv. no. 4490). Máire MacNeill Sweeney's marvellous bequest of paintings and drawings, which featured Picasso's *Still-life with Mandolin* (NGI Inv. no. 4522) and Juan Gris' *Pierrot* (NGI Inv. no. 4521), further added to the growing array of modern paintings. But it was in the domain of the old masters that the most significant addition was to be made, with a magnificent gift of seventeen paintings made by Sir Alfred and Lady Beit in 1987. The present exhibition contains no less than four works from this most splendid gift, *Kitchen Maid with the Supper at Emmaus* by Diego Velázquez, *The Marriage Feast at Cana* by Jan Steen, *The Castle of Bentheim* by Jacob van Ruisdael and *A Wooded Landscape - The Path on the Dyke* by Meindert Hobbema. The Irish taste for old master paintings lives on and it is safe to predict that they will continue to work their magic in Irish eyes into the twenty-first century.

Raymond Keaveney

CATALOGUE CREDITS

Catalogue entries are signed with initials and written by:

RK	Mr. Raymond Keaveney, Director, National Gallery of Ireland.
BPK	Dr. Brian P. Kennedy, Assistant Director, National Gallery of Ireland.
MW	Dr. Michael Wynne, Keeper, National Gallery of Ireland.
FC	Ms. Fionnuala Croke, Curator, National Gallery of Ireland.
ALH	Mr. Adrian Le Harivel, Curator, National Gallery of Ireland.
RM	Dr. Rosemarie Mulcahy, Lecturer, University College Dublin.

Photography by Mr. Michael Olohan.

HENDRICK AVERCAMP

AMSTERDAM 1585 - 1635 KAMPEN

Baptised in Amsterdam in January 1585, Hendrick Avercamp moved to Kampen in 1586, when his father, Barent, was appointed to the post of town apothecary. Some time later (c.1596), he moved back to Amsterdam, where he may have studied with the artist Pieter Isaacsz., who specialised in portraiture and history painting. In Amsterdam he would also have had the opportunity to study the works of painters from the Southern Netherlands, such as Gillis van Coninxloo and David Vinckboons, who had fled Antwerp to escape religious persecution. Their winter landscapes, and the compositions of Pieter Bruegel the Elder, were critical for his development. By 1613, he had settled back in Kampen, where he was to remain for the rest of his career, developing in paintings and watercolours the repertoire of winter landscape views of which he was the first and principal practitioner, his earliest examples dating from c.1608. Since he was dumb, Avercamp was known during his lifetime as 'de stomme van Campen'.

1 *Scene on the Ice,* c.1620

Oil on panel, 20.5 x 43.8 cm.
Signed: bottom left, with monogram, *HA*
NGI Inv. no. 496

Avercamp's winter scenes are amongst the most charming creations of seventeenth-century Dutch art. The origins of this seasonal genre are to be found in medieval manuscript painting which regularly included representations of the months, with images of December, January and February, each presenting views of winter life. This tradition found new expression in Flemish art of the sixteenth century, particularly in the compositions of Pieter Bruegel the Elder. Following the sack of Antwerp in 1576, many emigré Flemish artists brought their talent for rendering landscape north to the Netherlands, where it was quickly taken up and developed by local artists.

In this painting Avercamp presents yet another variation of his favourite theme, a canal scene in winter, populated with small figures either skating for pleasure or going about their daily business. The composition is flanked by a large, bare tree placed in the left foreground, with snow-covered houses bordering the canal to the right and left middle ground; a drawbridge in the centre frames the view of a more distant landscape. The sense of distance is enhanced through the modulation of the light, which is also skilfully employed to suggest the frosty atmosphere.

The drawbridge motif employed in the present painting is also to be found in another painting by the artist in The Hague (Mauritshuis, inv. no. 785) and in a drawing in Rotterdam (Museum Boymans van Beuningen, inv. no. H. 95). The figure seated under the tree in the centre foreground may be derived from medieval personifications of the month of February, whilst the dead carcass being devoured by a dog and carrion crows is probably a *memento mori.* Similar details are found in a painting by the artist which appeared on the art market in 1986 (New York, Sotheby's, Jan. 15, lot 30). The present painting has been dated to c.1620 by Blankert (1982) who considers the Hague composition to date to c.1610.

(RK)

POMPEO GIROLAMO BATONI

LUCCA 1708 - 1787 ROME

Born in Lucca, Batoni went to Rome in 1727, before he was twenty years of age. He was attracted towards the antique, and this influenced him to such an extent that his mature work could virtually be called Neoclassical. He painted altarpieces and history pictures. He is still best known for his numerous fine portraits of visitors to Rome, many of which show the sitters in classical settings either real or contrived.

2 *Joseph Leeson, afterwards 1st Earl of Milltown,* 1744

Oil on canvas, 137 x 102 cm.

Signed and dated: *Pompeo. Batoni. Pinse. Roma. 1744*

NGI Inv. no. 701 (Milltown Gift 1902)

Joseph Leeson (1711-1783) was a member of at least the fourth generation of a Dublin brewing family. He represented the borough of Rathcormac (Rathcormick), County Cork, in Parliament for several years. In 1756 he was created Baron Russborough, of County Wicklow; in 1760 he was made Viscount Russborough, of Russellstown, County Wicklow; in 1763 he was elevated as Earl of Milltown, County Dublin; and in 1770 he was made a Privy Councillor.

Leeson began the construction of his country house, Russborough, County Wicklow, in 1741, to the designs of Richard Castle; the house, one of Ireland's most elegant country mansions, was nearing completion in 1748 (*Georgian Soc. Records,* 1913). Fully restored to its pristine condition by Sir Alfred Beit, Bt., who bought it in 1951, it is now the seat of the Alfred Beit Foundation. Leeson also had a fine town house, no. 17 St. Stephen's Green, Dublin, now occupied by the Kildare Street and University Club. This house was built in the late 1770s.

In this portrait Joseph Leeson is wearing a fur-lined indoor coat. This item of clothing is found in many of Batoni's portraits, including that of Joseph Leeson's son, also Joseph (NGI Inv. no. 702, commissioned in 1751). Rome in winter can be very cold; while snow and ice are rare, a piercing cold wind, *la tramontana,* comes from the east and down from the Apennines.

This portrait was painted during Joseph Leeson's first visit to Rome, and must be among the earliest acquisitions of the Milltown Collection (Wynne 1974). As far as is known it is the earliest portrait by Batoni of any sitter from Great Britain or Ireland although a portrait of Arthur Rowley, destroyed by fire at Summerhill, County Meath, in 1922, was reputedly painted in 1740 (Russell 1982). Other members of the Rowley family were depicted by Batoni in portraits now destroyed; two small portraits of ladies of the Leeson family were executed, and happily survive (Clark 1985).

The Gallery possesses a copy of this Leeson portrait (oil on panel, 37.7 x 31.9 cm.: NGI Inv. no. 1648), probably made by an Irish artist, after the original Batoni was brought home.

(MW)

BERNARDO BELLOTTO

VENICE 1720 - 1780 WARSAW

Bellotto trained under his uncle, Canaletto, and followed in his footsteps as a view painter. Having visited and painted in several Italian cities, he emigrated, and is definitely recorded as being in Dresden in 1747, where he became a court painter to the Elector of Saxony. He made short visits to Vienna and Munich, and finally left Dresden for Warsaw in 1767. The King of Poland, Stanislaus Poniatowski, gave him many commissions. Outside of Italy, but particularly in Poland, Bellotto was also known as Canaletto, which has frequently given rise to confusion between the work of uncle and nephew, although their styles are quite distinctive.

3 *Dresden from the Right Bank of the Elbe above the Augustus Bridge,* c.1750

Oil on canvas, 51.5 x 84 cm.

NGI Inv. no. 181

4 *Dresden from the Right Bank of the Elbe below the Augustus Bridge,* c.1750

Oil on canvas, 51.5 x 84 cm.

Signed: bottom edge, centrally, *Bernard Bellotto dit Canaletto Peintre du Roi*

NGI Inv. no. 182

Dresden, the capital of Saxony, was destined to become one of Europe's most beautiful cities following the accession, in 1694, of Prince Elector Frederick Augustus I. By the time of his death in 1733 much had been done to beautify the city. He was succeeded in 1733 by his son Frederick Augustus II, who relentlessly pursued his father's policies. Both Electors welcomed artists to record the improvements, and the arrival in the city in 1747 of Bernardo Bellotto was very fortunate, since his exquisite view-painting was really actual and his treatment of buildings had architectural precision. For the Electoral Gallery he painted eighteen views of Dresden, and eleven of Pirna, a suburb of the capital.

The differences between the various versions of these views by Bellotto are very slight. In both cases the Dublin paintings show more than the others, and therefore are closer to the engravings of 1747, which are the work of Bellotto himself (Wynne 1986). It is necessary to examine the two paintings separately, since each is taken from a different viewpoint, one looking down the river, the other upstream.

Dresden from the Right Bank of the Elbe above the Augustus Bridge, beginning from the left hand side, shows, against the skyline, the great dome of the Protestant Church of the Virgin, completed to the designs of Georg Bähr between 1726 and 1743 (Hempel 1965). In front of the Church of the Virgin is a magnificent building, on the terrace (lowered fortifications) overlooking the Elbe. This, one of a series built by Heinrich Graf von Brühl, the prime minister, included a large assembly room, where visiting public officials and scholars could give lectures, or conduct colloquys. To the right, moving downstream, are further buildings built by Brühl, the last one here visible

being the Canaletto Room. At this point Brühl's property ends, in a boundary wall with the palace of the ancient Fürstenberg family; their palace overlooks the square at the end of the Augustus Bridge.

People are important in view-painting, to give a sense of scale, and in this picture several interesting individuals are identified by Walther (1990 Verona). In the foreground, in the very centre, are two artists: on the left, Christian Wilhelm Ernst Dietrich (1712-1774), a court painter from 1731, and on the right Johann Alexander Thiele (1685-1752), who, in a fourteen-year sojourn in Dresden, had painted many views, in a much more romantic style than Bellotto. To the right of the artists, in a group of three, are the Elector's physician, Filippo di Violante, the overweight contralto, Niccolò Pozzi, and the Turkish waiter. To the right of this trio is the court buffoon, Fröhlich.

In the complementary painting, *Dresden from the Right Bank of the Elbe below the Augustus Bridge*, the viewer is looking upstream towards the magnificent bridge constructed to the plans of Daniel Pöppelmann, between 1727 and 1731 (*Gemäldegalerie* 1979). The most prominent building in this painting is on the right hand side, the Roman Catholic Court Church. The architect was the Italian, Gaetano Chiaveri, and work began in 1738. The structure was not finished until 1755, when the tower, which owes much to Borromini and the Italian Baroque, was completed. To the right of the church, and behind it, one gets a glimpse of the much older palace of the Electors, with its famous Hausmann tower.

Kozakiewicz (1972) dates the Dublin Bellottos to circa 1750, Walther (1990 Verona) to 1748-50. Neither of these scholars, nor others consulted, offers any explanation as to why the artist anticipated the completion of the Court Church tower, especially when there are several Bellottos showing scaffolding on it.

(MW)

GIOVANNI BENEDETTO CASTIGLIONE

GENOA c.1610 - c.1665 MANTUA

A native of Genoa, Castiglione studied there under Giovanni Battista Poggi and Giovanni Andrea De Ferrari. Dissatisfied with his lack of success in his native city, Castiglione went to Rome where he worked for a picture dealer called Pellegrino Peri. Following an introduction to the Duke of Mantua, he was appointed a court painter and moved to Mantua in 1651, where he lived until his death. Apart from working for the Duke, he undertook commissions for other members of the Gonzaga family, and a variety of other patrons.

5 *The Shepherdess Spako with the Infant Cyrus,* 1650s

Oil on canvas, 234 x 226.5 cm.
NGI Inv. no. 994

Even by the time Herodotus (c.484-425 B.C.) wrote his famous *History*, the story of the early life of Cyrus had become entangled in legend; the most probable account is followed here. Cyrus was born to Mandane, a daughter of Astyages, king of Media (evidently by a god). Because of an oracle which foretold that Cyrus would overthrow his grandfather, the infant was given to a shepherd to be abandoned on a mountainside. The shepherd and his wife (whose name Spako means 'bitch') had lost their own child and decided to rear Cyrus in place of their recently dead son. Because of the literal meaning of the shepherd's wife's name, the myth grew that Cyrus was suckled by a dog; to the Persians, dogs were sacred animals. Cyrus grew up to be a great leader and conqueror, and the founder of the Persian Empire. Much of his success was due to the fact that he respected the traditions of the various peoples who made up the Empire, such as the Jews, the Medes, the Greeks and the Babylonians. Cyrus died in 528 B.C.

The Dublin painting is regarded as one of the finest and most beautiful works by Castiglione. As it was in Mantua in 1705 and relates to the *Deucalion and Pyrrha,* dated 1655, now at the Bodemuseum, Berlin, it seems very likely that it was painted during the 1650s, and as a specific commission. The statue of a man in the painting is almost identical to that in the *Deucalion and Pyrrha.* Castiglione painted the subject on at least one other occasion, and that canvas is now in the vestibule of the Palazzo Durazzo-Pallavicini, Genoa (Torriti 1967). The Durazzo-Pallavicini collection is one of the outstanding ones made by the great merchant-prince families of the Republic of Genoa (Cappelli 1930); it remains in the family to this day, and is protected by Italian state laws. Dublin is fortunate in having a magnificent Castiglione. He painted very grandly, and with relish, in his own way. He had an important influence on his son, Francesco, and on other painters, including the Spaniard, Pedro Orrente.

The Dublin painting was engraved by John Boydell on the basis of a drawing of it made by Richard Earlom. Published on 1 May 1765, an impression of the engraving, showing the composition in reverse, is in the NGI collections (Inv. No. 11, 943).

(MW)

JEAN~SIMÉON CHARDIN

PARIS 1699 - 1779 PARIS

Of the foremost artists of his generation Chardin is the only one who did not receive the thorough training offered by the Académie Royale. Although little is known of his early training, he enrolled in the less distinguished Académie de St. Luc in 1724 and undoubtedly spent time in the studios of Pierre-Jacques Cazes and Noël-Nicolas Coypel. He was admitted to the Académie Royale in 1728 as a 'painter skilled in animals and fruit'. Chardin worked slowly, carefully and painstakingly planning each composition; consequently his output was not great. Although his earliest works depict dead game and still-lifes he expanded his repertory to include, around 1730, scenes of kitchen interiors (as yet devoid of narrative), and from 1732-33 genre scenes and figure compositions. Chardin was a regular contributor to the Salons, which he was officially responsible for hanging from 1761. He received a royal pension from 1752, and five years later was granted living quarters in the Louvre, where he died at the age of eighty.

6 *Card Tricks (Les Tours de Cartes),* c.1735

Oil on canvas, 31 x 39 cm.
NGI Inv. no. 478

Chardin began to paint genre scenes around 1733; *Card Tricks* is one of a series of paintings by the artist in which playing cards are the focal theme. A young man has pulled up a chair at a table covered with a Turkey rug and is entertaining two young children with a card trick, evidently identifying the cards which he holds up with the face turned away from him. The caption on Surugue's engraving of 1744 reads 'You are beguiled, helpless youth, by these tricks you cannot take your eyes off; When you grow up, guard your heart from a thousand other tricks'. Although the playing cards can be read as allusions to *vanitas* and trickery, the appended verse lends a heavy moral tone to the image which it is unlikely that Chardin intended to convey. It is probable, however, that he did not oppose the verse, knowing that such a message would make for a more popular and thereby more profitable print.

This is the only surviving version of a number of known replicas of *Card Tricks*; it is not clear how many versions Chardin painted. A *Les Tours de Cartes* was exhibited at the Salon of 1739, and the Salon of 1743 included *Les Enfants faisant les Tours de Cartes*, possibly the same picture, with a pendant *Les Enfants qui s'amusent au Jeu de l'Oye*, both of which were engraved in reverse by Surugue in 1744. The National Gallery bought the present painting at the sale of Mme. de Bondy, the daughter of M. Moitessier. Bocher (1876), in his catalogue raisonné of engravings after Chardin, tells us that the *Tours de Cartes* then in the collection of M. Moitessier, *'provient de la vente de la liquidation de l'ancienne maison Giroux'*. The relevant part of the Giroux catalogue reads as follows: Monday, 10.2.1851. '*Vente de M. Alphonse Giroux. no. 39. Les Tours de Cartes.* [subject fully described. Surugue's engraving noted]. *Bois. H. 31 cm, L. 39 cm. Achetée 650fr par M. Moitessier'.*

The painter François Bonvin, writing to Laperlier on 8 February 1851, said of the Giroux painting: '... [it]must have been entirely repainted by a pretentious imbecile

who completely covered the master's work...'. Whether Laperlier bought the Giroux painting or not, a version of *Les Tours de Cartes* which had been in his possession since 1857 was included in the first sale of his collection. Bocher described the Giroux painting as on wood, but the present picture is on canvas and it was not transferred from panel to canvas. It may be that Bocher was mistaken. According to Wildenstein (1969) the Laperlier painting in the sale of 11-13 April 1867 (described as a sketch) was also on canvas.

The recent cleaning of this small painting revealed a paint surface in excellent condition and with no retouchings apart from a border added later (about 1 cm. top and bottom, and approximately 2.5 cm. on either side), so it is difficult to identify it with the picture described by Bonvin. The original paint surface corresponds exactly to the composition in Surugue's engraving. Although the painting differs in some details from that engraving - the folds of the youth's coat, cuff and pocket details, angle of the bookstand - the quality of the brushwork and the charming expressions of the enraptured little girl and puzzled young boy lead us to believe that this is another version by Chardin's own hand.

Yet another painting of this subject on canvas was recorded in the artist's estate inventory of 18 December 1779 (with its companion piece *Le Jeu de l'Oye*) and included in the Chardin sale of 6 March 1780, no.16. Wildenstein identified this painting with the Dublin picture. Wildenstein (1963/69) dated the Dublin painting c.1736, Rosenberg (1983a) to c.1734.

(FC)

CLAUDE LORRAIN

CHAMAGNE 1604/05 - 1682 ROME

Claude Gellée, called Le Lorrain, was born possibly in 1600 but more probably in 1604/05 (Kitson 1990). He first went to Rome c.1617, where he became assistant to a pastry cook, and at an undetermined date he began to work for Agostino Tassi (Sandrart). According to Baldinucci, he also spent two years with the Cologne painter Goffredo Wals in Naples. Resident in Rome from 1627, his earliest works drew on the landscapes of his teacher Tassi, van Swanevelt (who lived with Claude for a while), Breenbergh and van Poelenburgh. He also absorbed influences from Paul Bril and Adam Elsheimer. From around 1640, and continuing through the following decade, the great Italian classical painters became his foremost source of inspiration. From 1635 onwards he kept a record of each picture he painted in the form of a finished drawing, in a volume known as the Liber Veritatis. *He continued to paint up to his death, imbuing the work of his last decade with a lyrical, poetical quality.*

7 *Juno Confiding Io to the Care of Argus,* 1660

Oil on canvas, 60 x 76 cm.

Signed and dated: bottom, on a boulder, *Claudio IVF. Roma 1660*

NGI Inv. no. 763

Episodes from the *Metamorphoses* form one of the largest categories in Claude's art. His unspoilt landscapes provide ideal locations for these myths, imbuing them with the romantic and nostalgic spirit of the antique world. This small, late painting is his first represention of *Juno Confiding Io.* It was painted as one of a pair of pictures which remained together until 1805. Claude repeated the subject some years later in a larger picture of 1668, formerly in the collection of the Earl of Jersey (but destroyed by fire).

Ovid relates how Io, the daughter of Inachus, the first King of Argus, was seduced by Jupiter and then transformed by him into a white heifer to conceal her from his wife Juno. Juno was not deceived, however, and cunningly asked her husband for the heifer as a gift, which she then confided to the custody of Argus, the hundred-eyed giant. The pendant painting, *Mercury Piping to Argus* (sold Sotheby's, 27 March 1974, lot 63) portrays the subsequent episode in Ovid's story when Mercury charmed Argus to sleep with his lyre and cut off his head.

The artist has here subtly created a splendid landscape; although the foreground area is clearly defined by the imposing cluster of trees behind the trio of protagonists, the river conducts the spectator into the picture, and the bridge provides the link to the idyllic, classical town. While the theme of the picture may be tragic, the mood is charming and gentle; the grazing flock is munching contentedly, and the tiny figures dotting the landscape are happily unaware of the fate of Io. By portraying Argus as a young shepherd rather than the deformed giant of mythology, Claude has removed a potentially menacing element from his unflawed pastoral scene.

Sandrart reminds us that Claude, 'as a master of perspective ... knew how to break the hard quality of the colours and to mix them so that they no longer resembled those colours but what he wished to represent...'. Recent cleaning has emphasised the cold,

blue light of dawn coming from the left, playing on the water of the river Inachus and transforming the landscape, creating alternate areas of light and shade leading to the distant hills. The pendant, as is usual in Claude's companion paintings, is an evening scene lit from the right.

The pendant pair were recorded in the *Liber Veritatis.* The drawing for *Juno Confiding Io* (LV 149) corresponds exactly to the painting (Kitson 1978). Unfortunately the name of the patron is unclear on both drawings; the reverse of LV 149 is inscribed *Claudio G IV Roma 1660 faict pour m.Basont(?).* The pendant drawing of *Mercury Piping to Argus* is signed *Claudio IV Roma 1661* and inscribed on the back *Claudio Gelle IVF 1658 Roma faict pour m Boson ... (?).* In the first index for the *Liber Veritatis* the patron for LV 149 is given as 'Botteson'. This name has been variously interpreted. In his engraving of the drawing published in 1777 Earlom gave 'Batteson', and Pattison (1884) misread the name as 'Danton'. The name 'Boson', as read on the pendant drawing (LV 150), appears only once in the *Liber Veritatis* and was identified by Earlom as 'Bafont', and 'Bosout' by Pattison. Moreover, the first index of the *Liber* gives 'Lebrun' for LV 150 which Roethlisberger (1979) suggests is a confusion with LV 153. Nonetheless, there is no doubt that the Dublin picture and *Mercury Piping to Argus* were painted as a pair for the same patron.

(FC)

JACQUES~LOUIS DAVID

PARIS 1748 - 1825 BRUSSELS

Born on 30 August 1748, David initiated his study of painting under Vien in 1764 on the recommendation of Boucher, a relative by marriage, and two years later he entered the Académie Royale. He won the Prix de Rome *in 1774 and set out for Italy in 1775. By 1780, the date of his return to Paris, he had already conceived an articulate Neoclassical idiom. He was elected to the Académie in 1780 with* Andromache *(Musée du Louvre, Paris). Already successful as a portraitist, he lived in Rome again from 1784-85. Sympathetic to the Revolution, he became embroiled in Republican politics and played an active part in it and its aftermath; he led the attack on the Académie, which was abolished in 1793. When Napoleon came to power, David became his* premier peintre. *With the return of the Bourbons to power David fled to Brussels where he died in 1825.*

8 *The Funeral of Patroclus,* 1779

Oil on canvas, 94 x 218 cm.

Signed and dated: bottom left, *J.L. David f. Roma 1779*

NGI Inv. no. 4060

The reappearance of this extraordinary sketch in 1972 caused considerable excitement among art historians; a student work, it provides a missing link in David's development, from late Rococo painter to the emergence of his mature Neoclassical style.

The scene depicts the climactic close of Homer's *Iliad* (Bk. XVIII, vv. 110ff.). During the tenth year of the Trojan wars Patroclus assumed the guise of his friend Achilles to mislead the Trojans in battle. Patroclus was slain by Hector, son of Priam, King of Troy, and Achilles avenged his friend by killing Hector. The central motif of David's painting portrays Achilles mourning the loss of his friend on the raised bier, in front of the great funeral pyre which was ordered by Agamemnon. At the foot of the steps Hector's naked and twisted body is tied by the ankles to Achilles' chariot, where two rearing horses are ready to drag him around the city walls.

The diagonal shaft of light illuminating the central scene is halted by the oblique bulk of the pyre but highlights in its path a noble Trojan held on the bloodstained sacrificial altar, thus completing the triad of naked warriors who define the vacant foreground space. To the left, another prince of Troy is dragged to his death, while from the right sacrificial animals are led towards the pyre. The assembled multitude, estimated at 'more than one hundred figures' (Bouquier) represents the Greek camp, all of whom were present at the spectacular funeral, and in the distance the Greek vessels are anchored.

In a preparatory drawing (Musée du Louvre, Paris) for the *Funeral of Patroclus* the elements of the composition are already present, but the *traçes françaises* which David was later to regret in the oil sketch are more evident still in the Rococo deities in the heavens, intervening to protect the body of Hector. Significantly, in the later drawing in Honfleur (Musée Eugène Boudin), David has already abandoned the celestial

beings, lending prominence instead to the mortal heroes who have been brought forward to hold centre stage in the now frieze-like composition. A *pentimento* in the foreground of the National Gallery canvas, just to the right of the basin, seems to indicate that the artist had originally intended to place this vessel on a stand, as in the Honfleur drawing.

Exhibited first in the Palazzo Mancini in 1778 (despite being dated 1779; David may have retouched the picture a year later), the sketch was then sent to Paris to allow the Academicians to judge his progress. Although they perceived the promise of a 'prolific genius', the jury of the Academy noted the 'need to temper it and to tighten it in some way to give it more energy'. Their judgement was astute; the picture, painted with the rapidity of execution of a sketch, retains a baroque exuberance in the massing of disparate elements, with areas of flickering highlights contrasting with deep shadows.

When exhibited by David in his first Salon of 1781, the *Funeral of Patroclus* received favourable criticism (despite being badly hung). The critic in the *L'Annee littéraire* commented that 'if this painting were executed in relative proportion to the multitude of figures and the immensity of the scene, it would be unique in the world'. David, however, realised that by comparison with his other exhibits the sketch already seemed retrograde; Jules David (1880) recalled that in the winter of 1782-83 he used it as a support for a tabletop. Shortly afterwards he sold it to the collector and dealer Abraham Fontanel from Montpellier. The painting subsequently travelled to Naples, first to the Acton family, and then to the Serra, Duca di Cardinale collection. There is no further record of it until 1972. Rosenblum (1991) described its rediscovery in a Neapolitan collection as 'one of the great Eureka experiences of my life'.

(FC)

WILLEM DROST

ACTIVE 1652 - 1680

Few details are known about Willem Drost. Dated works by him are rare, the earliest being an engraved self-portrait of 1652; the latest is dated 1663. Arnold Houbraken, the early eighteenth-century art historian and painter, wrote that Drost studied with Rembrandt. Indeed, the style of Drost's dated works is similar to that of Rembrandt in the 1650s. Houbraken also states that Drost visited Rome with the painter, Joan van der Meer, and that while there he was associated with Johan Carl Loth, called Carlotto (1632-98). He went to Venice with Loth and it is known that he had returned to Holland by 1663. The last documentary reference to Drost is dated 1680. He painted biblical subjects, history scenes, individual allegorical figures and portraits. The excellent quality of Drost's major pictures has led to the attribution to him, in recent years, of some important works formerly attributed to his master, Rembrandt.

9 *Bust of a Man Wearing a Large-Brimmed Hat,* c.1654

Oil on canvas, 73.1 x 62 cm.
Signed: on right, centre, *W Dro(st)*
NGI Inv. no. 107

This strong, sensitively-handled portrait was attributed to Gerbrandt van den Eeckhout until 1982, when cleaning revealed the signature of Drost. C.E.W. Deacon (letter, NGI Archive) suggested that the picture may have been in the collection of Joseph Strutt of Derby, 'No. 163 Rembrandt, Head of a Jewish Rabbi'. There is, however, no evidence to suggest that the sitter is a rabbi. The man's costume is not unlike that in Rembrandt's *Self-Portrait aged Thirty-four* (National Gallery, London, cat. no. 672) and in the *Male Portrait* by Ferdinand Bol in Munich (Alte Pinakothek, inv. no. 609). It is likely that this costume, though not of the period, was a studio prop used by Rembrandt and his followers to dress their sitters and models.

Sumowski dated this portrait to about 1654, although he did not include it as by Drost. If this date is accepted, it means that the work was painted before Drost went to Italy. This is probable because the powerful influence of Rembrandt is obvious in the softened lines and the suffused light which creates an atmospheric aura around the head, and also in the rich colours and the effort to capture the character of the sitter. His gentle eyes and his intent, but somewhat perplexed, gaze convey a feeling of sadness to the viewer.

Drost, as noted by Sumowski, used the same model in *Man in Armour (Mars)* in Cassel (Gemäldegalerie, inv. no. 245), *Man in a Red Cap* in Dresden (Gemäldegalerie, inv. no. 1568) and *Seated Man with a Feather Beret,* formerly in the Rothschild Collection, which is dated 1654. Sumowski includes, as a related work, *Young Woman with a Feather Cap* in Cincinnati (Art Museum, inv. no. 1954:21); it is catalogued as by Bol but some experts have given it to Drost.

(BPK)

WILLEM CORNELISZ. DUYSTER

AMSTERDAM 1599 - 1635 AMSTERDAM

Son of a craftsman and minor city official, Duyster adopted his surname from the house on Koningstraat, 'De Duystere Werelt' (the dark world), where the family moved in 1620. By 1625 he was associated with the painter and dealer, Barent van Someren, when he is named on a document in a dispute with artist Pieter Codde. Codde was once thought to have taught him but they were in fact the same age; the portraitist and collector, Cornelis van de Voort, may have taught both of them. In 1631 Duyster married Margrieta Kick, sister of the genre painter Simon Kick, and Simon married Duyster's younger sister Styntge. Both couples then lived at the Duyster family home. Duyster died in the great Dutch plague of 1635.

10 *Interior with Soldiers,* 1632

Oil on panel, 48.2 cm. diam.

Signed and dated: lower right on middle step, in monogram, *WD 1632*

NGI Inv. no. 436

This is a typical Duyster subject, with soldiers off-duty in a barn. The central figure is accepted as a portrait of an officer, and his placing at the bottom of a short flight of stairs is identical to *An Officer* (The Mauritshuis, The Hague). The figure in The Hague is more obviously dressed as an officer, with his slashed satin sleeves, lace cuffs and bows at the knees and ankle, affectations mocked even at the time. There was no set uniform for the local troops or foreign mercenaries in the Dutch army and one has to gauge rank by the expense of the costume. The Dublin figure is more ambiguous than that in The Hague, but has an air of importance, while the finely rendered left figure, checking his leggings, exemplifies Duyster's sensitivity in recording a pose. Two seated figures behind could be gambling. There is a hunting bag on the wall.

Apart from the high quality of the brushwork in the principal figures and the detailing of the straw, the Dublin picture is interesting as the only known dated work by Duyster. The round composition demonstrates his interest in different picture shapes, and serves here to unify a scene where he typically concentrates the lighting equally on figures and still-life. A restricted palette reflects the Dutch liking for tonal painting from the late 1620s. Duyster's *oeuvre* is understandably small, predominantly of genre scenes with soldiers or fine company.

(ALH)

CONRAD FABER

CREUZNACH c.1500 - 1552 FRANKFURT

Born in Creuznach (today Bad Creuznach), a small town 40 miles west of Frankfurt, Conrad Faber moved to Frankfurt sometime before 1526, when he is recorded in the studio of Hans Fyoll. Faber concentrated on painting portraits for the local aristocracy, and about forty commissions have survived. In the early 1540s he was working at Lich for the Counts Solms, but he maintained his contacts with Frankfurt, having become a citizen of the city in 1538, and later secured the office of City Iron-Weigher. Despite frequently signing his works with his personal monogram (ƆvC), Faber's authorship of a large homogeneous group of portraits was not correctly identified until 1909, when Heinz Braune recognised the connection with the artist from Creuznach. Previously, a number of his works had been grouped together under the title of the Master of the Holzhausen Portraits, a group of paintings which included portraits of members of the Holzhausen family of Frankfurt.

11 *Katherina Knoblauch,* 1532

Oil on panel, 50.5 x 35.9 cm.

Signed and dated: on reverse, *ƆvC* (in ligature) *·M·D·XXXII·*

Inscribed on reverse, beneath coat-of-arms, *KATHERINA KNOBLAVCHIN YRES ALTERS·XIX· ·M·XXX·II·*

(Katherina Knoblauch her age 19).

NGI Inv. no. 21

Katherina Knoblauch (1513-1542) was the daughter of Johann Knoblauch and Katherina Gelthaus, members of the ruling House of Limpurg in Frankfurt. The word Knoblauch means garlic in German and this plant, the family emblem, is the dominant feature in the coat-of-arms on the reverse of the painting. In 1529 Katherina married Friedrich Rohrbach, six years her senior, and three years later Faber executed a pair of pendant portraits of Katherina (NGI Inv. no. 21) and her husband (Chicago, Art Institute, inv. no. 1935.296). The two pictures remained joined together as a diptych until the Farrer sale of 1866, when the present picture was acquired for the collection. The sitters wear elaborate costumes, that of Katherina being especially brilliant with its fine fabrics and an abundance of gold embroidery and jewellery.

Faber has set the couple against a continuous panoramic landscape which forms a seamless backdrop to both paintings. The alpine mountains, the lake, the small island and the foreground details span both pictures. Such fantastic landscapes are a feature common to almost all of Faber's portraits, and most probably derive from Netherlandish and Middle-Rheinish models. Following a trip to Passau around 1532, his later works also show the influence of the Danube School.

Purchased as by Georg Pencz, the work was listed in early Gallery catalogues as by the Swiss artist, Hans Apser. In the 1908 catalogue, it was attributed to the 'Master of the Holzhausen Portraits'. Attribution to Faber was confirmed in the 1928 catalogue; Braune (1909) had noted the relationship some years earlier. The Gallery possesses two other portraits by the artist, one of Heinrich Knoblauch (NGI Inv. no. 243, signed and dated 1529), the brother of Katherina, and another of an unidentified man (NGI Inv. no. 804), an early work.

(RK)

THOMAS GAINSBOROUGH

SUDBURY 1727 - 1788 LONDON

Gainsborough showed early talent and came to London in 1740 to study with the French engraver Hubert Gravelot. He returned to Sudbury in 1748 as an accomplished landscapist, but only assured with small-scale portraiture. He moved to Ipswich in 1752 to increase his clientele, then from 1759 worked in Bath. Here he graduated to life-size scale and closely studied the old masters. He exhibited in London from 1761 and was a foundation member of the Royal Academy in 1768, but began exhibiting in his home at Schomberg House after a quarrel over hanging in 1784. Considered second only to Reynolds in his lifetime, his approach to portraiture was more spontaneous and, unusually, he painted his own draperies. Gainsborough's late landscapes and 'fancy pictures' are increasingly romantic.

12 *A View in Suffolk,* c.1746

Oil on canvas, 47 x 61 cm.
NGI Inv. no. 191

This delicate early Gainsborough landscape of chalk pits by a pool blends features of his native Suffolk with elements from Dutch seventeenth-century landscape paintings. The structure here of low horizon, winding cart track, high banks and brooding clouds echoing the landscape below can be traced to Ruisdael. The dramatically-lit centre and windswept trees also recall Ruisdael. Gainsborough's intention, though, is more decorative, akin to French Rococo painting in the patterning of the clouds. This is combined with sharply observed details such as the sturdy peasants, the water trickling into the pool and the barking dog in the middle distance. The face of the chalk pits is richly worked (imitating the approach of Berchem) and there are also echoes of Wijnants, whose *Landscape with Horsemen and Peasants* (1665, National Gallery, London) is a similar composition. The jutting tree and seated man with a pole are also common to Wijnants, as is the silvery grey tonality, painted over a light ground colour.

A View in Suffolk is remarkable in that for all the borrowed ideas, Gainsborough successfully evokes the spirit of his native county. He no doubt worked from drawings such as *Study of a Sandy Bank* (National Gallery of Scotland, Edinburgh), though none of the early painted landscapes records any specific view. Even the church tower seen in the Dublin painting is imaginary, and not Dedham church as was once thought. The picture belongs to a small group of landscapes from shortly before his first actually dated one, *Rest by the Way* (1747, Philadelphia Museum of Art). There Gainsborough shows his increased understanding of both Ruisdael and Hobbema, with a more monumental feel, closer integration of figure and landscape details and attention to the effects of changing weather.

(ALH)

ORAZIO GENTILESCHI

PISA 1563 - 1639 LONDON

Born in Pisa, a son of goldsmith Giovanni Battista Lomi, Orazio initially studied painting with his elder brother, Aurelio Lomi, and with his uncle Bacci Lomi. In 1576 or 1578 Orazio moved to Rome, staying with a maternal uncle, Captain Gentileschi, whose family name he adopted. He is first recorded as a painter when working under the direction of Cesare Nebbia in the Biblioteca Sistina, in the Vatican, in 1588-89. He continued to paint in a not very notable way, until he saw some of Caravaggio's work. From about 1605 his own personal style emerged and he produced some very distinguished work. Invited to Genoa, he painted several large canvases; from Genoa he was called to Turin to work for the Duke of Savoy; having returned to Genoa to work for the Sauli and Doria families, he was invited to Paris by Maria de'Medici, in 1624. In 1625 he was invited to London by Charles I to be a court painter, and remained there until his death in 1639. Several of Gentileschi's works remain in the Royal Collections to this day.

13 *David and Goliath,* c.1605-06

Oil on canvas, 185.5 x 136 cm.
NGI Inv. no. 980

The biblical story of David and Goliath is told in Chapter 17 of the *First Book of Samuel.* Goliath, one of the great warriors of the Philistines, offered to fight any man from the troops of the Israelites. King Saul and his senior advisers were terrified, but David came forward, and went out to meet Goliath, armed with his sling and five stones. With the first stone he knocked Goliath to the ground, having hit him in the middle of the forehead. David ran forward, took Goliath's sword, and then cut off Goliath's head. The Philistines, dismayed, fled.

The attribution to Gentileschi is unequivocal. Longhi (1943) suggests a date at the beginning of the second decade of the seventeenth century, which seems eminently reasonable given the striking Caravaggesque qualities of the painting. Wittkower (1973) writes that it 'must have been created in Rome at an early period of his career'. Both of these would agree with Emiliani's date of c.1610 (1958). Bissell, in his major monograph on Gentileschi (1981), places it within the years c.1605-10.

This painting has no direct prototype in the known works of Caravaggio. Gentileschi was definitely influenced by Caravaggio's work; however, Caravaggism was only one component in his mature personal style. Recently (1991) Luciano Berti said about the painting exhibited here: 'Some of his [Gentileschi's] compositions on an oblique composition, such as *David and Goliath* in Dublin, with vibrant thrust and whirling cut, in a tempestuous atmosphere, make one think of sculptures by Francesco Mochi (another person born on the banks of the Arno)'. Schleier (1962) has made a most interesting proposal by comparing the Dublin Gentileschi with the artist's *St. Michael* altarpiece in the Church of San Salvatore, in Farnese (Viterbo). The artist probably made a small version some years before the final altarpiece (Bissell 1981). Benedetti has proposed that *David and Goliath* was executed 1605-06 (1992 Dublin).

(MW)

BARON FRANÇOIS~PASCAL~SIMON GÉRARD

ROME 1770 - 1837 PARIS

Gérard was born in Rome, but the family returned to Paris in 1780. Studying first with the sculptor Pajou (from 1782) and then with the painter Brenet (from 1784), Gérard entered the studio of David in 1786 and became one of the principal portraitists to the imperial court of Napoléon I. He first attracted attention in the Salon of 1795 with his Bellisarius *(formerly in the collection of the Leuchtenberg Gallery, Munich). From 1800 he received a flood of important commissions to paint the Emperor and his family. After the fall of the Empire, under the Bourbons, the artist was appointed* Premier Peintre du Roi *to Louis XVIII, and was made a baron in 1819. Although he was troubled by deteriorating sight and health from about 1820, Gérard painted until his death in 1837.*

14 *Julie Bonaparte as Queen of Spain with her Daughters, Zénaïde and Charlotte,* 1808-09

Oil on canvas, 200 x 143.5 cm.
Signed: lower right, *F. Gérard*
NGI Inv. no. 4055

Marie Julie Clary (1777-1845) was the elder daughter of a wealthy Marseilles family, reputedly of Irish descent (Leahy 1968). Her sister, Desirée, became engaged to Napoléon Bonaparte at the age of fifteen while his younger brother Joseph wanted to marry Julie. Although the engagement between Napoléon and Desirée was eventually broken off, Julie married Joseph Bonaparte on the 14 Thermidor Year II (1 August 1794). Her large dowry, probably exceeding 150,000 francs, saved the Bonapartes from penury and allowed Joseph the means to pursue his political career. Their daughter Zénaïde was born in 1801 and Charlotte the following year. In 1806 Joseph became King of Naples. Julie, however, remained in Paris with their daughters, only joining her husband at the very end of his reign in April 1808. In that year Joseph was named King of Spain, a title he held in name until 1814.

This is one of five portraits painted by Gérard, at the height of his power, for Napoléon's *Salon de Famille* of the Palais de Saint-Cloud. Its commission is recorded in two letters from the Duke of Frioul, the first to Faget de Baur (15 September 1808) and the second to Vivant Denon on 25 September (Latreille 1989). Gérard has portrayed Julie as Queen of Spain, seated by the window in a gilt empire chair with Zénaïde on her right and Charlotte on her left. The setting, with the view of the pond and trees, is thought to be the château of Mortefontaine, Joseph's residence outside Paris. Gérard's highly polished finish faithfully renders the textures of the little girls' muslin and voile dresses and Zénaïde's satin shoes. Their mother wears a white satin dress decorated with gold lamé foliage. The border of stylised foliage at the hemline is repeated on the red velvet overcape which is let in at the bodice. A very similar cape is found on a dress which belonged to Julie and was probably designed by Leroy, and which is today conserved in the collection of the Marquise della Chiesa, née Roccagiovine (Hubert 1976). The long-sleeved dress in Gérard's portrait is, however, a ceremonial gown; the cape is held at the shoulders by narrow straps and the shoulders

are finished with transparent fairy-ring epaulettes.

Presumably the painting hung at Saint-Cloud until the fall of the Empire. By 1818 (de l'Ain 1970) it was back in Gérard's studio where he supervised a copy to be sent to Julie in Frankfurt. Gérard also repaired the damage caused by Prussian troops who slashed the portrait, notably the Queen's face, with their sabres. Joseph arrived in New York in August 1814; he lived in America as the comte de Surviliers, dividing his time between Philadelphia and the farm at Point Breeze which he had bought on the banks of the Delaware. He remained there until 1832 when he travelled to London, returning to America from 1837 to 1839. Julie meanwhile retired first to Frankfurt and later to Brussels where her two daughters had their portrait painted by David (1821, Museo Napoleonico, Rome).

The painting hung in the grand salon of Joseph's home at Point Breeze alongside Gérard's portraits of Napoléon and Joseph (de l'Ain 1970). It may have been sent out in 1836 with several other pictures as it is listed under that year in the *'Etat des tableaux que l'on doit emporter en 1836'* (Bertin 1893). It is included again in an inventory drawn up by Joseph himself ('no. 113, "*La Reine Julie et les Princesses.* Gérard." Valued by the King at the high figure of 12,000fr.') (Bertin 1893).

Zénaïde married her cousin Charles-Lucien Bonaparte, eldest son of Lucien Bonaparte and Alexandrine de Bleschamp, in 1822 and had twelve children. Her younger sister was married in 1826 to another German cousin, Napoléon-Louis, son of Louis Bonaparte and Hortense de Beauharnais. According to family papers (Ansaldi 1955) the picture was inherited by Zénaïde, and remained with the family until 1972.

(FC)

FRANCISCO DE GOYA Y LUCIENTES

FUENDETODOS (ZARAGOZA) 1746 - 1828 BORDEAUX

At the age of fourteen Goya entered the studio of the painter José Luzán in Zaragoza, where he spent four years. His marriage in 1773 to Josefa Bayeu, sister of his teacher Francisco, marked a turning-point in his career. Through Francisco he gained access to the court circle in Madrid, where he settled in 1774, and became painter to the king in 1786. In the winter of 1792-93 Goya, aged forty-six, was struck by a serious illness which left him stone deaf. This crisis released a darker and highly creative vein in his work, which found expression in his first series of etchings, the Caprichos *(published 1799). During the following decade, he painted some of his greatest masterpieces and the Napoleonic invasion of Spain (1808-12) provoked a powerful series of etchings, the* Disasters of War. *A second, almost fatal, illness in 1819 resulted in the disturbing* Black Paintings, *with which he covered the walls of his newly acquired villa on the outskirts of Madrid, the Quinta del Sordo. Against the troubled background of the tyrannical rule of Ferdinand VII, he departed for France in 1824, finally settling in Bordeaux.*

15 *'El Conde del Tajo'*, c.1800

Oil on canvas, 62.5 x 52.5 cm.
NGI. Inv. no. 600

In this engaging portrait the sitter is shown half-length, wearing a grey wig, brown jacket and embroidered cravat. When purchased in 1908, the portrait carried a label which referred to the subject as *El Conde del Tajo.* The title is not listed in any of the standard directories of Spanish nobility and the identity tag may be spurious. The portrait was illustrated in the 1924 edition of the Zapater letters, where the identity was given as 'unknown'.

Critical opinion is divided regarding the portrait's authenticity. Many experts have accepted it, but Gassier and Wilson excluded it from their catalogue raisonné of Goya's *oeuvre.* Wilson Bareau (letter, NGI archive) believes that the *Conde* 'is fundamentally too dry and tight in style and handling to qualify as a Goya, even allowing for possible damage', and points to 'the lack of softness and subtlety in the brushwork' and 'backbone' in the sitter's pose.

In format this work compares with the portrait of *Meléndez Valdés* (Bowes Museum, Barnard Castle, Durham), which is signed and dated 1797, although the brushwork in the latter is softer. In the Dublin portrait the hard outline of the left side of the face is disturbing, as is the pedestrian overall treatment of the jacket, for which there is no parallel in Goya's *oeuvre.* However, the modelling of the face and the almost challenging directness with which the *Conde* meets the viewer are worthy of Goya and in spite of the doubts expressed about the portrait's authenticity, the attribution to him is maintained here. The double-breasted jacket suggests a date in the early nineteenth century.

(RM)

JAN DAVIDSZ. DE HEEM

UTRECHT 1606 - 1683/84 ANTWERP

De Heem is the finest of a dynasty of still-life painters. His father, David de Heem I, initially taught both him and his younger brother David II. Jan Davidsz. de Heem was apprenticed to a leading Utrecht still-life painter, Balthasar van der Ast, who strongly influenced his early work up to c.1623. He worked in Leiden from 1625 to 1636, where he was influenced by Rembrandt, and married in 1626. In 1636 he moved to Antwerp and joined the Guild of St. Luke. He remarried in 1644. From 1669 to 1672 he returned to Utrecht, but following the French invasion of Holland again moved to Antwerp, where he died between November 1683 and April 1684. Sons from his two marriages, Cornelis and Jan Jansz. II, and a grandson, David, continued the family tradition.

16 A Vanitas *Fruit-piece,* 1653

Oil on canvas, 85.5 x 65 cm.
Signed and dated: on the ledge, *J- De Heem f. Ao 1653*
NGI Inv. no. 11

De Heem first painted *vanitas* groups, but with books and skulls, under the influence of Rembrandt in Leiden. The earliest is dated 1625. In Antwerp he painted mainly fruit and flower groups and, possibly influenced by Frans Floris or Adriaen van Utrecht, developed the sort of garland or hanging bouquet seen here. This is an outstanding example, with the added interest of the *memento mori* symbolism conveying the underlying meaning that man's Salvation is through the Passion of Christ. The lifecycle is shown by the fig (fall from grace), youth (relief of children), adulthood (crucifix) and death (skull). Christ on the crucifix symbolically rises over the devil (snake) and mortality (skull and fly). The caterpillars which become butterflies, and corn that dies, then is reborn, symbolise resurrection. An Admiral butterfly is contrasted with the central magpie moth. The cherry is the fruit of paradise, also symbolised by the blue ribbon holding the garland. The grapes will become the communion wine in the rummer glass, and the children are harvesting for the communion bread. The pomegranate is both Christ and the Church, and the plum signifies fidelity.

The first major de Heem exhibition (1991 Utrecht and Braunschweig) gathered several versions of the Dublin composition. Cornelis de Heem practically copied it in 1654, and a similar bouquet hangs in a large banquet-piece by Jan Davidsz. de Heem (more like a Snyders), from the 1660s (Academy, Vienna). There the *vanitas* theme is only hinted at. It is again explicit in a collaborative reworking of the Dublin composition in 1672 (Alte Pinakothek, Munich).

(ALH)

MEINDERT HOBBEMA

AMSTERDAM 1638 - 1709 AMSTERDAM

Hobbema was the great master of the picturesque wooded landscape painting. He was baptised in Amsterdam on 31 October 1638 as Meyndert Lubbertsz, but adopted the name Hobbema when he was a young man. Jacob van Ruisdael testified in 1660 that Hobbema had been his apprentice for 'some years'. Hobbema's earliest pictures are not particularly impressive, but following his years with van Ruisdael, his art developed and he produced many large-scale landscapes, the best known of which is The Avenue, Middelharnis *(National Gallery, London), painted in 1689. Hobbema's entire career was spent in Amsterdam. He married in 1668 and became one of the wine-gaugers of Amsterdam, a post he retained until the end of his life. He died in Amsterdam on 7 December 1709.*

17 *A Wooded Landscape - The Path on the Dyke,* 1663

Oil on canvas, 105.5 x 128 cm.
Signed and dated: bottom, towards the right, *Meyndert Hobbema f. 1663*
NGI Inv. no. 4533 (Beit Collection)

Hobbema's early work was much influenced by his master, Jacob van Ruisdael. In about 1662, however, Hobbema began to paint larger and more ambitious pictures, breaking free from van Ruisdael's influence. Wright has emphasised the importance of this development: 'He branched out on his own to become the real inventor of the picturesque wooded landscape'.

This picture is generally regarded as Hobbema's masterpiece and was so described in 1835 by Smith who found 'terms of description insufficient to give a correct idea of the superlative beauty and excellence of this *chef d'oeuvre* of Hobbema'. Smith wrote that the picture represented 'a rural scene, in which industry has triumphed over local difficulties, and from a marshy bog created a luxuriant landscape'. In 1857, Waagen declared the picture to be 'the masterpiece of Hobbema, both for extent and for excellence; a picture which is equal to a whole gallery ... For striking truth of nature, delicacy of aerial perspective, effect of a bright afternoon sun, and masterly lightness of execution, there are probably very few pictures in the world which can bear a comparison with this'. The picture's reputation has been sustained in this century, most recently by Sutton (1987) who described it as Hobbema's 'indisputable masterpiece ... which, like his other works of 1663, introduces a new variety into his design, offering a view of a high road on the right separated by a group of tall trees in the centre from a low pathway and pond beneath it on the left'.

Nearly all of Hobbema's pictures emphasise trees and heavy foliage. He was a specialist but, within the confines of his narrow subject range, his views demonstrate versatility and imagination. Although the places in his views are not generally identifiable they all show, as in this painting, superb analytical precision in their detail which has obviously been studied from nature. The contrast between the bright sky and the dense vegetation and dark water creates a feeling of overall stillness, but the scene is enlivened by the peasant figures and animals. Two drovers have stopped to

have a conversation with a shepherdess who is seated by the roadside. A man and a woman are strolling on the path beside the dyke below the road, and a man is fishing in the pond. Smith considered that these details were painted by Adriaen van de Velde, who often collaborated with Hobbema, and this view has been endorsed by Bode and Sutton. Hofstede de Groot thought that the figures were probably by Hobbema but that the animals were 'in the style of A. van de Velde, perhaps by Dirck van Bergen'. Sutton has noted the stylistic similarities between this painting and the Hobbema landscapes in the Taft Museum, Cincinnati (inv. no. 1931, 407) and in the Musées Royaux des Beaux-Arts, Brussels (inv. no. 2616).

(BPK)

WILLIAM HOGARTH

LONDON 1697 - 1764 LONDON

Hogarth first trained as a silver engraver but by 1720 was producing satirical prints. He married the daughter of history painter Sir James Thornhill in 1728 and was soon busy painting theatrical scenes and conversation pieces. The Harlot's Progress *(1732) was his first successful engraved series of moral subjects, followed by* The Rake's Progress *(published in 1735 after he had ensured the passing of the Act of Copyright) and others. In spite of professing a dislike for everything foreign, he twice visited France (and was famously arrested in Calais as a spy) and attempted Italianate history painting for the Foundling and St Bartholomew's Hospitals. In the 1740s Hogarth painted his most ambitious portraits, and he published* The Analysis of Beauty, *a treatise on aesthetics, in 1753.*

18 *The Mackinen Children,* 1747

Oil on canvas, 180 x 143 cm.
NGI Inv. no. 791

The sitters, William Mackinen (1733-1809) and his sister Elizabeth (1730-1780), were identified only recently (Webster 1989). They were the grandchildren of Daniel Mackinen (1658-1720), younger son of the clan chief on the Island of Skye, who emigrated from Scotland to the West Indies. He received a grant of land on the Island of Antigua and his son William (c.1697-1767) became a wealthy landowner. He married Charity Yeamans and the children here were their eldest. In 1752 Elizabeth became the second wife of Dr Thomas Fraser and died on the Island. In 1757 William married Louisa Vernon (1738-1816) from a Staffordshire family, and inherited his father's estate of over 830 acres in 1767. They had eight children. William was a member of the Council from 1764 to 1798 when he resigned his seat and returned with his wife to England. They lived at Binfield, near Windsor, in Berkshire, which was thought in the past to be the view shown in the picture. In 1808 he became 32nd chief of the Scottish clan.

Hogarth must have painted *The Mackinen Children* when they came to complete their education in England, as was customary for wealthy families abroad. Family tradition records that it was painted in 1747 when Elizabeth was seventeen and William was fourteen. The children are attracted by the butterfly on the sunflower, leaving aside things of permanence (the book and shells) for passing beauty. The sunflower, placed at the centre of this enclosed world, is also a reminder of the tree of knowledge in the garden of Eden. The terraced house behind them is imaginary.

Some have doubted that this painting is by Hogarth, but *The Graham Children* (1742, National Gallery, London) shares its scale and theme. The composition here is a little awkward because of the central placing of the sunflower, and the figure drawing is weak in places, but this may be because only the children's heads were painted from life. An x-radiograph of William's head confirms Hogarth's hand, together with the overall conception, the use of his serpentine line of beauty in Elizabeth's pose, the fabric painting, the dog, and even the elaborate flowerpot design. For all the robust

handling of the faces and details, there is a certain French elegance in the gestures that shows the imprint of Rococo art at this date. Colouring is muted, with characteristic olive green in the background, other shades of green in William's waistcoat and the sunflower leaves, and a pale violet in Elizabeth's dress and the sky. The brightest area is significantly the sunflower. There appears to have been a vogue amongst the nobility for children's double portraits with similar imagery around 1740 (by Ramsay, Dandridge and others), which Hogarth may have wished to emulate.

A boy's portrait by Gainsborough (Gainsborough House, Sudbury), long asserted to be William Mackinen, is now known to be from a quite different double portrait.

(ALH)

WILLIAM HOGARTH

19 *The Western Family,* c.1738

Oil on canvas, 72 x 84 cm.

Signed and dated: lower right, *W Hogarth 173.. Pinx*

NGI Inv. no. 792

Thomas Western (1714-66) of Rivenhall, Essex, is shown arriving home to take tea with his wife Anne Callis (d. 1776), mother, daughter and either the Reverend William Hatsell or Archdeacon C. Plumptre. A servant has appeared with a letter for the clergyman. There has been some confusion over the sitters, as the earliest description (Nichols 1781) mentions 'four clergymen', and a Reverend William Cole claimed to be the man in the background (Mss., British Museum), but this figure is clearly dressed as a servant and putting the cover on a gun. Hogarth also painted Thomas Western alone in 1736, the year he married (untraced). *The Western Family* was painted around 1738, like the similar *Strode Family* (Tate Gallery, London). The signature appears to have been strengthened, with the last digit of the much lighter date now covered by the P of 'Pinx', so that it cannot be read.

Thomas Western's pose is more appropriate to a hunting scene, as he presents a dead bird to his mother (in Dutch art a lewd proposal), still wearing his hat indoors. The Westerns have an English harpischord (strings shown back to front), a painted screen of a house and walled garden, a gilt mirror, and one picture, an overdoor of dead game in the style of Fyt. The tea-table appears to be solid silver, rather than silvered wood, as in *Assembly at Wanstead* (c.1731, Philadelphia Museum of Art). The porcelain tea service and silver pot reflect the expense of tea and the ritual then associated with drinking it. Such family scenes were first popularised by immigrant artists like Mercier and van Aken in the 1720s, and were a staple of Hogarth's work for a decade from 1729.

(ALH)

WOLF HUBER

FELDKIRCH c.1485 - 1553 PASSAU

Wolf Huber was born in Feldkirch in the Vorarlberg region of Western Austria, where he may have had his first training in the studio of Hans Huber, possibly a relative, who headed a workshop there at the end of the fifteenth century. Around 1505 he travelled to Innsbruck, Salzburg, and possibly Vienna and Augsburg, making drawings as he travelled. By 1515, however, he appears to have settled in Passau on the Danube, where he remained for virtually the rest of his career, employed by Ernst of Bavaria and the Bishop of Passau. His earliest documented painting is the St. Ann Altarpiece, commissioned for his home town of Feldkirch, which he delivered in 1521; in this work, his evident love of nature echoes the work of his great contemporary, Albrecht Altdorfer. Apart from continuing to supply altarpieces for churches in Passau and elsewhere, and developing his skills as an observer of landscape through his sketching of the landscape scenery he viewed on his travels, Huber also worked as an architect. In 1529 he was appointed court architect to Nicholas II of Salm, count of Neuburg am Inn (15 miles from Passau), and in 1541 he became city architect in Passau.

20 *Anton Hundertpfundt,* 1526

Oil on panel, 68.6 x 47.6 cm.
Inscribed on marble plaque, *ANTTAI·HVNDERT// / //PFVNDT·IST ALLT / ·51·IAR·DA MAN· /* Z[ÄLT]·*1526 J*[AR] / *WH* (Anton Hundertpfundt is 51 years old as one counts)
NGI Inv. no. 15

Anton Hundertpfundt, *Munzmeister* (mint-master) to Wilhelm IV, Duke of Bavaria, was a member of a prosperous family whose ancestors had served in the Bavarian treasury since 1435. According to Habich (1908-09) the clothes he wears here are possibly his official robes of office. This portrait was originally flanked by the companion portrait of Anton's wife, Margaret, now in the Philadelphia Museum of Art (John G. Johnson Coll., inv. no. 1438). The tradition of producing pendant portraits of husband and wife was well established in Germany at this time (see Faber, Cat. no. 11). Huber, who was exceptionally talented at depicting landscape, has, in the case of Anton and Margaret Hundertpfundt, chosen to set his subjects against an unusual background of unfinished masonry, possibly reflecting his talents as an architect, though the device may also have some symbolic significance. In this confined, almost claustrophobic, setting, possibly a courtyard, he has identified his subjects by setting inscribed plaques into the side walls giving the name of each sitter and the date of the commission.

The circumstances behind Huber's commission for the Hundertpfundt portraits have yet to be explained. Local artists, such as Hans Wertinger, were the most frequently employed for court portraits. Oldfield (1987) has suggested that Huber may have been in Munich at the invitation of Wilhelm IV, to discuss a series of history pictures which he was planning at about this time and for which Altdorfer painted the magnificent *Battle of Alexander and Darius* (1529, Alte Pinakothek, Munich). Such a journey would have given Huber the opportunity to paint Anton Hundertpfundt and his wife.

(RK)

ANTTAÏ·HVNDERT·
PFVNDT·IST·ALLT
·5·IAR·DA·MAN
Z·1526
WH

MATHIEU LE NAIN (ATTRIBUTED TO)

LAON c.1607 - 1677 PARIS

The problem of distinguishing the three separate hands of the brothers Antoine, Louis and Mathieu Le Nain continues to intrigue scholars, despite the illuminating exhibition organised by Thuillier in 1978. All three lived together until the deaths of Antoine and Louis in 1648; they signed their works without either first name or initial and, moreover, they collaborated on some paintings. However, since 1978, a number of proposals have sought to divide up the work of the Le Nains into three homogenous groups, as a result of which a group of paintings can be ascribed to Mathieu with a relative degree of certainty.

Mathieu was in Paris with Antoine and Louis in 1629. In 1633 he became both Peintre Ordinaire de la Ville de Paris *and* Lieutenant de la Compagnie Bourgeoise du Sieur du Ry. *All three brothers attended the first assembly of the Académie Royale on 1st March 1648. Mathieu's assumption of the title* Sieur de La Junelle, *the name of his small farm near Laon, would seem to attest to his social ambition. In 1662 he received the coveted* Ordre de Saint-Michel, *which honour he was obliged to renounce in 1666. He died in 1677.*

21 *Adoration of the Shepherds,* 1644

Oil on canvas, 59 x 67 cm.

Signed and dated: on a beam at lower right, *Lenain f. 1644*

NGI Inv. no. 1645

When the Dublin *Adoration of the Shepherds* came to light in 1923 in the Dr. Mary collection, the date was deciphered as 1674, and it was consequently attributed to Mathieu Le Nain, the only brother alive at that date. When the painting was exhibited in 1934, Waterhouse and Sambon suggested that the date might be read as 1644, and subsequent cleaning confirmed their reading. The attribution was promptly changed to Louis, the most talented of the brothers. This authorship was sustained when the picture was purchased by the Gallery in 1961, and maintained in all subsequent Gallery catalogues. However, three related studies by Cuzin (1978 and 1979) and Rosenberg (1979b), arising out of the 1978 exhibition, have led to the identification of Mathieu's artistic personality, and both scholars have convincingly included this picture among the works they, independently, ascribe to him.

This small canvas portrays the shepherds and their families coming to adore the Christ Child in a realistic and humble manner. The landscape setting is stony and uncomfortable, the buildings ruined and inhospitable. A variety of figures has gathered around the young Virgin and her son, lying in a makeshift cradle of wood and straw. While the central figures, including the old woman and the Caravaggesque figure of a kneeling, bearded shepherd, focus their attention on the Child, the unconnected, wandering stares of the attendant figures in this silent world create a disjointed mood, and only the young boy standing at the back meets the spectator's eye. Though the picture is slightly damaged, having suffered from overcleaning sometime in the past, the palette of greys and browns, lifted by the use of a brighter blue and red, retains much of its original appeal.

(FC)

FILIPPINO LIPPI (ATTRIBUTED TO)

PRATO 1457 - 1504 FLORENCE

The son of the artist Fra Filippo Lippi, Filippino Lippi spent the early years of his life in Prato, where he received the first part of his artistic education in his father's workshop. Following Fra Filippo's death in 1469, Filippino moved to Florence and completed his training under Botticelli, whose influence heavily characterises his early work. In the mid-1480s he executed a number of important works for Florentine patrons, including an altarpiece representing the Vision of St. Bernard *for the Church of Campora at Marignolle near Florence (Florence:Badia). In August 1488 Filippino was called to Rome by Cardinal Oliverio Caraffa to decorate the family chapel in Santa Maria Sopra Minerva, where he covered the walls with a series of frescoes which are characterised by a fascination with the world of the antique and a quality of disquiet which will later find fuller expression in the art of the mannerist painters. Back in Florence by 1493, he continued to attract important commissions, the most notable being the cycle of frescoes for the Strozzi chapel in the Church of Santa Maria Novella, Florence. In his final years, with his reputation growing, he worked for patrons in Bologna, Prato and Genoa as well as Florence.*

22 *Portrait of a Musician,* 1480s

Oil and tempera on panel, 51 x 36 cm.
Inscribed: lower left, *e ichonjcar no fia p tempo mai* ('and it will never be too early to begin')
NGI Inv. no. 470

The identity of the sitter in this portrait remains unknown, though an old label, since lost, erroneously referred to the subject as Angelo Poliziano (1454-1494). However, the features of the great poet and humanist are well known to us (Hill 1951) and cannot be said to resemble the sitter in the present work. Most probably a noted poet-musician of the period, the young man is shown tuning a *lira da braccio,* at that time considered the most noble solo instrument and used widely to accompany recitations of poetry. The almost snapshot immediacy of the image is striking and novel. Portraiture at this time was expanding from a concentration on noble subjects, who had no need to define their profession, to include a wider clientele, who required that the image in some manner illustrate their professional status, broadening the scope of the traditional portrait to involve an almost *genre* - like quality. The influence of this change is visible in the present work, in the representation of the various objects which fill the shelves in the left background on which there rest a lute, another *lira da braccio* and two small wind instruments, possibly recorders, together with some sheets of music.

Regarding the authorship of this portrait, Sergio Ortolani once commented 'it is a picture without a home, perhaps because it has had too many'. Certainly a great deal of ink has been spilt in speculation over the last century or so as to whom the artist might have been, and it has been variously attributed to artists from Florence, Ferrara and Lucca, including Raffaellino del Garbo, Botticelli, Ercole de'Roberti, Francesco del Cossa, Cosimo Tura, Baldassare d'Este, Lorenzo Costa, Francesco Francia, the Master of the Lucchese Immaculate Conception and 'il pittore di Paolo Buonvisi'. On a recent visit to the National Gallery Federico Zeri repeated his earlier support (1974)

for an attribution to Lippi, commenting that the difficulty which many scholars have had in recognising his authorship can be put down, to some extent, to the abraded condition of the panel, in part a direct consequence of Lippi's technique. Alfio del Serra (1985) has noted the master's use of mixed media, combining tempera and oil, and his preference for finishing his works with a large amount of egg white varnish, a procedure which has tended to make many of his pictures low and dark in tone. Because the concentrated varnish used by Lippi was applied to the still fresh paint, its removal almost inevitably involved damage to the picture, as in this instance.

As already noted, it has not proved possible to identify the subject of this intriguing portrait. That Lippi was a skilled portraitist is well documented by the many superb likenesses he inserted into his great fresco cycles and subject pictures, most notably his work in the Brancacci Chapel in Florence; however, few portrait commissions by his hand have been identified, and the present work must represent an important example. Stylistically the work would appear to date to the early 1480s, around the time of the *Vision of St. Bernard*, where the face of the saint is delineated in a similar fashion, and where there is still the fascination with the representation of details of the real world as made popular in the paintings of the Northern masters, such as Memlinc and van der Goes. The work may have been done for a patron in Bologna, a city visited by Lippi in 1501 when he received a commission for the church of San Domenico. According to Andrea Bacchi (written communication, October 1991) the portrait may well be that documented by Oretti as in the collection of the Aldrovandi in Bologna in the eighteenth century, which corresponds closely in description to the present work. A wax seal on the back of the panel displays the coat of arms of the Boncompagni Ludovisi family, a distinguished family of Bologna who also had properties in Rome, where the painting was documented prior to its acquisition.

(RK)

ANDREA MANTEGNA

ISOLA DI CARTURA c.1430 - 1506 PADUA

Born in the village of Isola di Cartura, not far from Padua, Mantegna moved to that city c.1440 to start an apprenticeship (till 1457) with Francesco Squarcione. His master was an artist of only modest accomplishment, however, and the young Mantegna must have gleaned much of his knowledge from his study of the works of other masters which were available in and around Padua, particularly those of Donatello, who was active there for a period of ten years (1443-53). Other influences would have been Filippo Lippi, Andrea del Castagno, Jacopo Bellini and Antonio Vivarini. By 1447 Mantegna was undertaking independent commissions, and one year later he was employed, along with three other artists, to decorate the Ovetari Chapel in the Church of the Eremitani (destroyed, 1944) where he demonstrated his extraordinary skills in perspective and the archaeological enthusiasms of his patrons. His reputation established, he began to attract the attention of some of the foremost patrons of the day. In 1456 he supplied an altarpiece for the Church of San Zeno, Verona, one of his most inventive and influential commissions. By January 1457 he had agreed to enter the service of Federigo Gonzaga in Mantua, moving there in 1459, and he continued to work for Gonzaga till his death, producing, among other brilliant works, the frescoes for the Camera Picta.

23 *Judith with the Head of Holofernes,* c.1495-1500

Distemper on linen, mounted on millboard, 48.1 x 36.7 cm.
NGI Inv. no. 442

During the Renaissance, four hundred years before the establishment of the modern Italian Republic, the Italian peninsula consisted of a web of independent states, many of them small and vulnerable. This situation is reflected in numerous artworks of the period, in images which portray the triumph of individuals or small states against more powerful enemies. The present painting, which takes its subject from one of the canonical books of the Old Testament, belongs to this tradition. The image depicts the delivery of Bethulia (*Judith,* ch. 13, vv. 9-10) from the control of its powerful enemy, the Assyrians, through the heroic action of Judith, the widow of Manasse of the tribe of Ruben. When the powerful Assyrian army, under their general, Holofernes, laid siege to the city of Bethulia, all seemed lost until the pious Judith succeeded in gaining entry to the camp of the enemy and decapitating Holofernes with his own sword as he slept. Apart from its obvious historical meaning, such a story would have been interpreted by Renaissance commentators as illustrating the triumph of virtue over vice and the victory of the weak over the powerful. In a purely religious context, with its female heroine, it would have been seen to prefigure the Virgin. This bloodthirsty subject, with its topical symbolism, obviously held a great fascination for Mantegna and his patrons, as he depicted the subject on numerous occasions in drawings, prints and paintings.

The present painting is one of a number of works by Mantegna which are painted in *grisaille* to imitate classical relief, in either stone or bronze. Lightbown (1986) suggests that the artist first thought of developing this particular approach to easel painting in the 1490s, possibly as a less expensive form of decoration for his clients who, in any

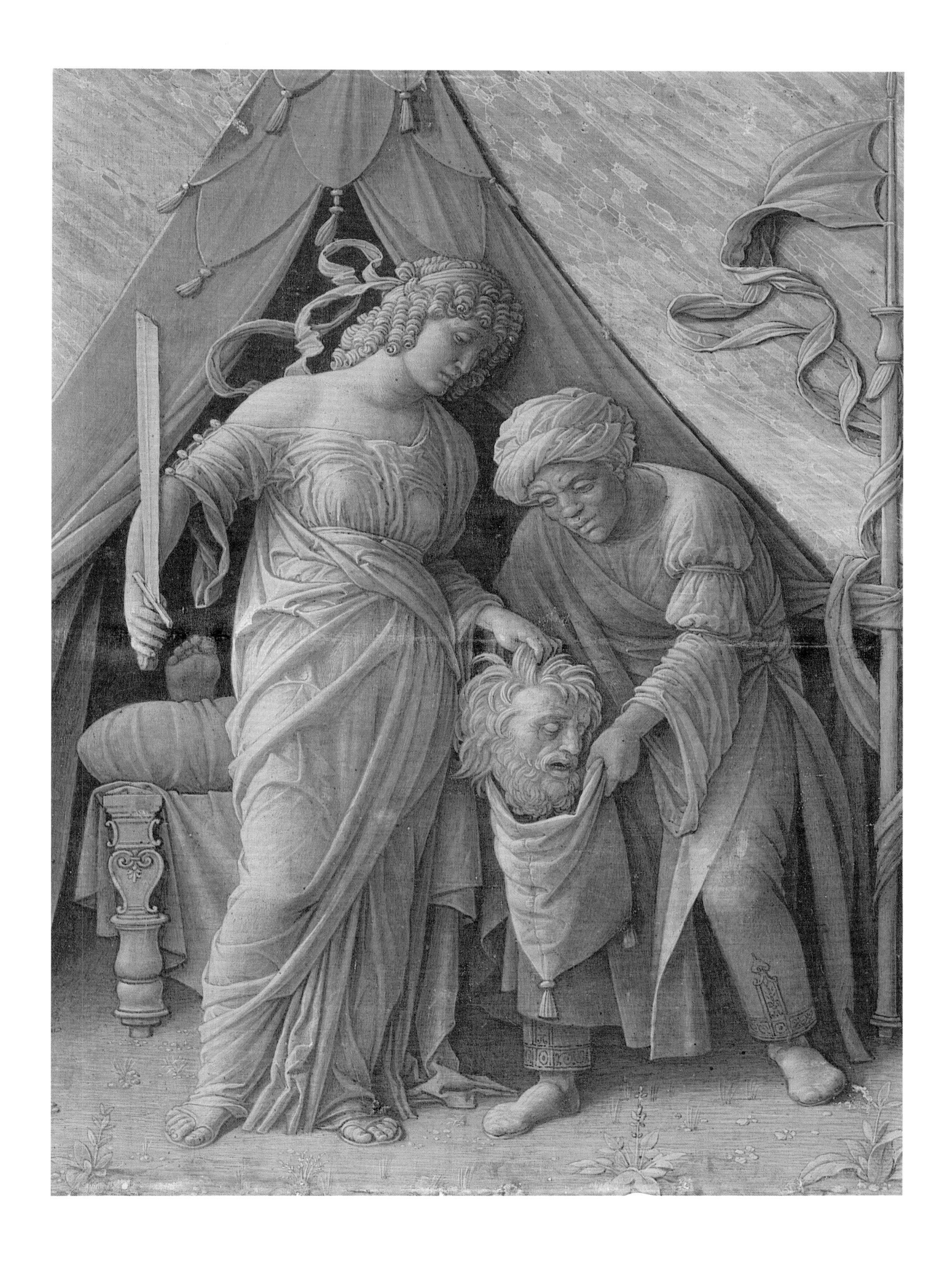

event, would have had difficulty in obtaining antique originals or finding local sculptors with the talent to supply contemporary imitations. Mantegna is known to have created two decorative schemes involving such paintings, one of which included the Old Testament figure of Judith, the subject of the present painting. His most remarkable achievement in this technique is his large canvas showing *The Introduction of the Cult of Cybele in Rome* in the National Gallery, London, painted in 1505-06.

The attribution of the present work to Mantegna is virtually unanimous among modern critics, though there has been much debate regarding the painting's authenticity in the past. For Oberhuber (1966 and 1973) the Dublin painting is the master's finest rendition of the Judith theme. Christiansen (1992) notes that many of the reservations expressed about Mantegna's authorship of the work may have been due in part to the fact that most critics knew it only from reproduction. He claims that a careful study of the work itself, with the aid of magnification, reveals the hand of the master in the delicacy and precision of the details. He believes the painting may be related to the London *Samson and Delilah,* which also has a black border framing the composition, and similar fold damage. The two works may originally have formed part of a cycle of paintings illustrating some theme in which women played the central role.

(RK)

ANTON RAPHAEL MENGS

AUSSIG (BOHEMIA) 1728 - 1779 ROME

Mengs showed outstanding artistic ability from an early age, and at twelve he was taken to study in Rome. He particularly excelled in portraiture, both in pastel and oil, and gained the patronage of Augustus III of Saxony, who made him Court Painter at Dresden in 1745 and gave him a pension to study in Rome. He was appointed Royal Painter in 1751 but from the following year he made his home in Rome, where his vivid and elegant style of portraiture attracted a large clientele, and he became a celebrated exponent of Neoclassicism. In 1761 he was called to Spain by Charles III, former King of Naples; he worked in Madrid as Court Painter from 1761 to 1771 and again from 1773 to 1777. Mengs was appointed director of the Royal Academy of San Fernando in Madrid; he also acted as artistic advisor to the royal tapestry factory of Santa Barbara.

24 *Thomas Conolly,* 1758

Oil on canvas, 135 x 98 cm.
Signed: *Ant. Raff. M... Sassone*
NGI Inv. no. 4458

This elegant painting portrays Thomas Conolly (1739-1803), son of William Conolly MP and grandnephew of William Conolly, Speaker of the Irish House of Commons and builder of Castletown, County Kildare, one of the finest neo-Palladian mansions in Ireland. Like many young men of his privileged class, Thomas Conolly went to Rome to finish his education, and it was there in 1758 that this portrait was painted.

The young man is portrayed three-quarter length against the monumental base of a Doric column, which establishes a mood of classical *gravitas.* He wears an elegant dark blue coat, and a jacket which is trimmed with gold braid and shows heavy white lace at the wrists and throat. The sculptural frieze, to which he draws our attention, is a reminder of the educational purpose of his visit to Rome. While in his early twenties Mengs had already perfected this type of strongly modelled portraiture and he continued to use it, with variations, during the rest of his career. This ability to endow his sitters with a regal elegance explains, in part, his large clientele of Grand Tourists. The sculptural relief which is given prominence in Conolly's portrait is taken from a sarcophagus, now in the Louvre, and shows three of the nine Muses, who represented the highest artistic and intellectual aspirations. Mengs was to re-use the figures from this relief in the *Parnassus* in the Villa Albani a few years later. Although Calliope (epic poetry), Urania (astronomy) and Melpomene (tragedy) are represented here, Conolly is not known to have excelled in any of these. In fact he appears to have been an unremarkable young man, except for his large fortune and a tendency to tell very bad jokes. Conolly seems to have brought back no other significant works of art from his Italian trip, apart from a signed replica of his portrait.

(RM)

GIOVAN BATTISTA MORONI

ALBINO c.1520/24 - 1578 ALBINO

Giovan Battista Moroni was born c.1520 in Albino, a small town some 8 miles from Bergamo, in the Val Seriana, where his father, Francesco, was an architect. He most probably entered the studio of Moretto in Brescia by 1532 and trained with the master until about 1544. After a brief spell working in Brescia alongside Moretto, he began to seek work elsewhere, including his native Albino and in Trent, where he worked on and off till 1553 during the first two sittings of the Council. It may have been at this time that he viewed Titian's work, as there is no record that he ever visited Venice. In the late 1550s he expanded his clientele, winning commissions from the pro-Spanish aristocracy in Bergamo. In 1562 he settled back in his native Albino. He is best known for his portraits, a discipline in which he is recognised as being one of the supreme masters. The full-length canvases date mostly to the 1550s and 1560s with the more complex, three-quarter length seated compositions dating to the later part of his career.

25 *Portrait of a Gentleman and his Two Children,* c.1565

Oil on canvas, 125 x 97 cm.
Inscribed: '... *Albino* ...'
NGI Inv. no. 105

Despite the fact that the sitter's name may originally have been legible from the inscribed letter placed on the table to the left of the composition, the identity of the subject in this sensitively managed portrait has puzzled the critics down through the years. When sold at Christie's (14 May 1858, lot 32) it was identified as a portrait of the writer Pietro Aretino (1492-1556) with his children. Later Cook (1915b) proposed Hamilcar Anguissola and his children as the subjects, while others have proposed it as a portrait of the artist, due to the inscription identifying the setting as Albino, which was Moroni's home town. It has also been titled 'Portrait of a Widower and his Two Children'.

The painting, a haunting image of parenthood and paternal tenderness, is unique in Moroni's *oeuvre,* as the artist did not normally paint group portraits nor is he known to have executed many portraits of children. Against a beautifully modulated slate grey/blue background, the father, dressed in a dark costume with narrow white ruffs, is shown embracing his two brilliantly-clad daughters. The setting is Albino, as indicated by the inscription in the letter which rests on the table to the left. Moroni had returned there from Bergamo around 1562, and at this time the influence of the sober Spanish dress, which is evident in the costume of the father, had replaced the more flamboyant local attire which had been the norm until the late 1550s. Another sobering influence was that of the Council of Trent (1545-63) which had set itself the task of reforming the Church.

Moroni's responsibility for this intimate portrait group has not always been acknowledged, though his authorship now stands unchallenged. Lerndorff (1939) viewed the painting as exhibiting the traits of the Brescian School, and argued, on stylistic grounds and type of costume, that the painting should be dated with Moroni's works of the mid-1560s, an assessment shared by many critics, most recently Gregori (1979).

(RK)

JAN MYTENS

THE HAGUE c.1614 - 1670 THE HAGUE

Jan Mytens, a fashionable portrait artist active in The Hague in the mid-seventeenth century, studied with his uncle Daniel Mytens the Elder and was the father and teacher of Daniel Mytens the Younger. His many patrons included Dutch government officials, their families and the rich merchants of the capital city. He became a member of the Guild of St. Luke in The Hague in 1639 and helped to found a confraternity of painters there in 1656 known as 'Pictura'. Daniel Mytens the Elder had worked in England at the court of Charles I and was influenced by the Flemish masters, Rubens and van Dyck. This influence was passed on to Jan Mytens by his father.

26 *A Lady Playing a Lute,* 1648

Oil on canvas, 79 x 63 cm.

Signed and dated: top right, *Mytens pincxit 1648*

NGI Inv. no. 150

Waagen described this picture in 1854 as 'Mytens - a female portrait with a guitar'. The music historian Barra Boydell has noted that, in fact, the lady is playing a 'theorboed' lute. This instrument has two distinct pegboxes and was popular with French lute composers, so much so that it was known in England as the 'French lute'. Despite Mytens' apparent attention to detail, the number of strings does not correspond to the number of pegs.

Although the portrait was exhibited in 1882 as a *Portrait of the Countess of Derby,* and sold in 1889 as *Charlotte de la Tremouille, Countess of Derby Playing a Guitar,* there is no evidence to support this identification. The lady bears no resemblance to the Countess of Derby as painted by van Dyck in a family portrait now in the Frick Collection. A painting of *Minerva* by Gerrit van Honthorst, signed and dated 1652 (sold at Christie's, 4-5 June 1984, lot 471), which bears an inscription identifying the sitter as Charlotte de la Tremouille, is also quite unlike the lady playing a lute in our picture.

The huge number of extant Dutch seventeenth-century portraits is evidence of the economic and political stability of the Netherlands during that century. The new, prosperous, middle class in particular was eager to record its social elevation by commissioning portraits. Artists often had fixed prices which were related to the size of the picture required and to the number of individuals to be portrayed.

It is probable that this portrait was painted with a pendant of the lady's husband. A man would typically celebrate an engagement or marriage by commissioning pendant portraits of his fiancée or wife and himself. The lute is often used in art to symbolise harmony and, consequently, it was considered appropriate to paintings of married couples. Mytens painted a number of pair portraits of married couples. His ability to capture a likeness and his consummate handling of draperies account for his popularity as a portraitist.

(BPK)

Mijtens pinxit. 1648

JEAN~BAPTISTE PERRONNEAU

PARIS 1715 - 1783 AMSTERDAM

According to the registers of the Académie Royale, Jean-Baptiste Perronneau, student of Natoire and of Laurent Cars, the engraver, was born in Paris in 1715, and died in Amsterdam in 1783, aged sixty-eight. He was listed by the Académie in 1746 as a 'peintre de portraits', *and elected a full member in 1753. Perronneau travelled in France and later to Italy, visiting England in 1761, Russia in 1781, Poland in 1782, and making numerous visits to Holland between 1754 and 1783, when he died there. He did not receive patronage from the aristocracy, and although he exhibited at almost all the Salons between 1746 and 1779, he was forced from 1754 onwards to seek out a new clientele and thus spent the remainder of his life travelling.*

27 *Portrait of a Man,* 1766

Oil on canvas, 72.5 x 58.5 cm.
Signed and dated: top right, *Perronneau 1766*
NGI Inv. no. 920

This portrait of an unknown man in early middle life, signed and dated 1766, was purchased by the Gallery in 1929 from Agnew's, London. A possible key to his identity is the sheet of paper he is holding which is inscribed *Agriculture, Arts et Commerce,* but no sustainable identification has been proposed. The portrait was not known to Vaillat and de Limay when they published their fine monograph on the artist in 1923, nor do they describe an engraving that corresponds to the sitter. Agnew's bought the picture in London, and said that the previous owner told the firm that it came from a private collection in the South of France, regrettably without supplying them with the name of that collection. The artist travelled a great deal in France, and it is possible that this man of the arts, agriculture and commerce came from (and indeed sat for Perronneau in) the South.

The pose of this distinguished gentleman - half length, seated in three-quarter view with his head turned towards the spectator - is one which the artist repeated in a number of portraits. Perronneau was best known as a pastellist, and this painting captures something of the fragility and softness of finish of a pastel portrait. The subtle tonality and neutral background - relieved by the loosely but carefully painted white lace of his shirt, and the glimpses of freer brushwork in his brocade waistcoat - draw the viewer to the steady clear gaze of the sitter. The light, coming from the upper left, models his face and falls down to his hand, where the slip of paper records his achievements. The features are painted with fine brushstrokes, defining the straight nose, thin mouth and fuller chin, while broader sweeps of paint capture the velvet texture of his jacket. Perhaps the appeal of this portrait lies in its simple, understated realism and quiet dignity.

(FC)

agriculture,
arts.
et commerce.

NICOLAS POUSSIN

LES ANDELYS 1594 - 1665 ROME

Poussin is celebrated as the greatest French painter of the seventeenth century. In his own lifetime he was sought out by the French monarch, and French collectors (Richelieu, Chantelou, Pointel) fought over his works. Born in Les Andelys (Normandy) in 1594, he trained in Rouen and Paris, but his works from this early period are lost. By 1624, at his third attempt, he arrived in Rome. Except for a reluctant and unhappy trip to France at the summons of Louis XIII, from 1640-42, he never left Rome again. Following his first important large-scale commissions, Poussin applied himself exclusively to cabinet paintings for a select circle of educated and highly cultured patrons. In 1630 he married Anne-Marie Dughet, sister of the painter Gaspard Dughet. From 1630 his works are characterised by an increasing classicism. From the 1650s onwards there is a greater interest in landscape in his work.

28 *The Holy Family with Saint Anne, Saint Elizabeth and the Young Saint John,* called *The Virgin with Ten Figures,* 1649

Oil on canvas, 29 x 106 cm.
NGI Inv. no. 925

The Holy Family was painted in 1649 for Jean Pointel, silk merchant and friend of the artist (Félibien 1725). After the merchant's death in 1660 it was listed in an inventory drawn up by Philippe de Champaigne (Thuillier and Mignot 1978), described as 'another painting likewise on canvas without frame three feet long by two and one-half feet wide upon which is the subject of the Virgin holding the Infant Jesus, Saint Joseph, Saint Anne with the baby Saint John, appraised at the sum of four hundred livres...'. The picture was bought by the silk merchant Jacques Cérisier (Thuillier and Mignot 1978), at whose Paris home it was seen by Bernini in August 1665 (Chantelou 1885).

Until 1826 (Neale) there is no further mention of the painting; in that year it was listed in the earliest known inventory of the collection of the Earls of Milltown, hanging in the Saloon of Russborough House, outside Dublin. That collection was formed in the eighteenth century by the first Earl, Joseph Leeson (Wynne 1974). The Milltown papers remain untraced; however, a purchasing trip to Paris may be sustained from a study of Neale's list, which includes around twenty-five paintings by French artists. *The Holy Family* was subsequently presented to the National Gallery as part of the Milltown Gift of 1902.

The portrayal of Joseph, the Virgin and the Christ Child together with Anne, Elizabeth and the infant John is a scene of popular devotion and has no biblical precedent. Poussin favoured this theme, painting a number of variations on it during the late 1640s and 1650s, several of which are in US collections. There is a preparatory drawing for the Dublin canvas in Chantilly (Musée Conde, inv. 304) which differs in a number of respects from the finished work. Perhaps most important is that in the painting Poussin has controlled the directional gazes, focusing the attention of Joseph, Anne and Elizabeth on the figure of the Virgin. The immobile,

statuesque quality of the figures, their solemn expressions and the apparently inward gaze of the Virgin herself emphasise her role as the Eternal Mother.

The grouping of the Holy Family, in particular the figure of the Christ Child balanced on his mother's knee with his arms outspread, relates closely to a drawing in Stockholm (National Museum, C.R. 32). The playful angels paying tribute to the Child are found again in the *Holy Family with Nine Figures* (Fogg Art Museum, Cambridge) dated 1650 (Rosenberg 1982) and the *Holy Family with Eleven Figures* (jointly owned by the J. Paul Getty Museum, Malibu and the Norton Simon Museum, Pasadena) of 1651 (Mahon 1962). Related to the putti of Roman sarcophagi, the figure of the first angel carrying a basket of flowers on his head may be compared to the putto carrying a basket of grapes from the mosaics in Santa Costanza, Rome. The background view of a town seems to contain memories of a journey by the artist in Tuscany, notably the Lucchese-Romanesque tower on the left (behind the figure of Joseph), with its crenellation and blind arcading, and the porched house on the right, so similar to a country *pieve* (church), decorated with the usual 'della Robbia' type majolica.

There is a copy of the *Holy Family* in San Francisco (The Fine Arts Museums of San Francisco; Rosenberg and Stewart 1987). The Dublin painting has not escaped without some doubts as to its authorship but Blunt, who exhibited the San Francisco painting in 1960, later declared the Dublin version as original, reaffirming his opinion in his catalogue of 1966. D. Mahon (1961) agreed with the attribution of the Dublin canvas, and was left in no doubt after the cleaning of the picture in 1962, which revealed a pentimento in the head of St. Anne, and the bold, acid colours. More recently Laveissière (1985) accepted it as 'evidently the painting executed for Pointel in 1649'.

(FC)

NICOLAS POUSSIN

29 *The Lamentation over the Dead Christ,* 1655-60

Oil on canvas, 94 x 130 cm.
NGI Inv. no. 214

The subject of the Lamentation, although depicted frequently in European paintings between the fifteenth and seventeenth centuries, is not described in the Gospels; it was a development from the Byzantine images of the Entombment, gradually expanding to include the figures of the Virgin and St. John, and has its root in the apocryphal Gospel of Nicodemus (Weitzmann 1961).

Poussin's painting was, in fact, referred to as the *Entombment* in National Gallery catalogues from 1885-1983. Joseph of Arimathea, who took Christ's body and 'wrapped it in a clean linen sheet', already kneels in the entrance to the tomb, at Christ's feet. But the painting depicts more correctly the moment, however brief, after the embalming of the body, and just prior to the placing in the tomb, when Christ's mother and a few of his disciples reflect on and grieve for his death. St. John raises Christ's head on to his lap, about to fold his left arm over his chest, in order to wrap the body in the white sheet. Mary Magdalen kisses his hand and behind her is the 'other Mary' (both are mentioned by Matthew and Mark). The jar and basin refer to the anointing with 'myrrh and aloes to preserve the body' (*John* Ch. 19, v. 39).

The expression of grief is largely concentrated in the upright figure of the Virgin, holding her cloak to her face. Standing apart, not touching her son's body, she presents, not the immensely suffering mother, but rather her acceptance of the sacrifice of her son for the salvation of man. Her role, underlined by the gesture of surrender she makes with her left hand, signifies the message of the steadfast strength of faith in the imminent Resurrection. Behind her the stark tree, bearing new shoots, further alludes to the new life, the regrowth which follows the Resurrection.

Poussin's restraint in conveying each figure's sense of grief serves to heighten the spiritual intensity of the image. The drama is further increased by his choice of striking, rich colours. Cloaked in deep, intense blue, the Virgin affirms her role; the Magdalen's shot orange robe seems to reflect her violent sense of loss; while the vibrant red around Christ's head pronounces him as the spiritual centre of the painting. Each figure is enveloped in his/her own particular sense of loss; the stark elemental landscape, with the city in the left distance providing the historical reference, plays its own part in this contained manifestation of sorrow.

Certain points of reference have been recognised. The figure of Christ was inspired by Sebastiano del Piombo's *Pietà*, painted for the church of San Francesco in Viterbo (now Museo Civico), which in turn was based on a drawing by Michelangelo. The vertical, heavily draped figure of the Virgin was, meanwhile, borrowed from an engraving after Raphael by Marcantonio Raimondi.

Although Grautoff (1914) dated the *Lamentation* 1643-48, other writers (Blunt 1960a,

exh. cat., 2nd ed. and 1966; Mahon 1960 and 1962; Thuillier 1974) have agreed on a date in the late 1650s. The National Gallery painting is therefore the work of an artist in his sixties who was suffering increasingly from ill health. It may be compared with an earlier *Lamentation* by the artist of c.1629 in Munich (Alte Pinakothek; for summary of dating see Oberhuber 1988). The swooning figure of the Virgin and the gesticulation and movement in the earlier painting serve to emphasise the detachment and immobility, and moreover the psychological penetration, which the artist achieves in the mature work. Poussin's attitude to death in the 1650s is very different from that of almost thirty years earlier. In this late painting he has conceived the *Lamentation* as a meditation and reflection on death; and in so doing, he has succeeded in creating one of his most poignant and memorable images.

(FC)

MATTIA PRETI

TAVERNA IN CALABRIA 1613 - 1699 VALLETTA

Still in his teens Preti went to Rome, and from there travelled extensively throughout northern Italy. It is very difficult to get precise details of these travels or to find dated works. By the 1640s he was back in Rome where a number of documented commissions are to be found, mostly frescoes in churches. In the mid-1650s he went to Naples, and about 1660 moved to Malta where he remained for the rest of his life. His best known works are those which manifest a strong interest in chiaroscuro, and dark tonalities.

30 *The Beheading of Saint John the Baptist,* c.1640

Oil on canvas, 135 x 97 cm.
NGI Inv. no. 366

St John, already bound, still manages to hold the shaft of his cross, around which is tied the ribbon with the letters *E.A.D.E.*, an abbreviation of his primary proclamation: *Ecce Agnus Dei; ecce ...* (Behold the Lamb of God; behold ...). The figure to the left behind St. John is presumably one of Herod's courtiers, clerical or lay. He is wearing a head-dress with stripes, a type that recurs frequently in Preti's paintings, for example in *Christ Raising Lazarus* in the Pinacoteca at Naples or *Christ and the Canaanite Woman* in the Museo Nazionale at Palermo (Taschetta 1959).

This picture came to the Gallery as a Caravaggio and was catalogued under this name until 1971. The attribution to Preti is absolutely convincing, but it is not easy to date with precision. Undoubtedly it is a work of his maturity, probably painted during his years in Naples before he went to Malta in 1660. The tranquillity, the clarity, the dignity, and the plain background of the Dublin painting are attributes not readily found in Preti's *oeuvre.* The rather different painting of *Two Philosophers* in the Pinacoteca Capitolina, Rome, does have some of these qualities, as does *The Liberation of St. Peter,* in Vienna (Chimirri and Frangipane 1914). John T. Spike (1981 letter, NGI Archive) proposes a somewhat earlier date of circa 1640, grouping it with such works as *St. Catherine of Alexandria Visited in Prison by the Empress* in the Dayton Art Institute, Ohio, and *The Crucifixion of St. Peter,* in the Musée, Grenoble. Recently, focusing on the influence of Caravaggio on Mattia Preti, Sergio Benedetti wrote: '.. the profile of the executioner with his morion, leaving only the nose and the beard exposed... seems to have been suggested by the *St. Ursula* painted by Caravaggio for Marc Antonio Doria, which we know was in Genoa at least until 1651' (1992 Dublin). The *St. Ursula* Caravaggio is now the property of the Banca Commerciale d'Italia (on deposit with the Museo di Capodimonte, Naples). The Genoese commission for the Caravaggio is significant for the Preti exhibited here; in the NGI Archives are notes which indicate that the Preti belonged to the Marchesi Cambiaso, Genoa, but the documentation is not adequate enough to make this fact absolutely certain (Wynne, 1986).

(MW)

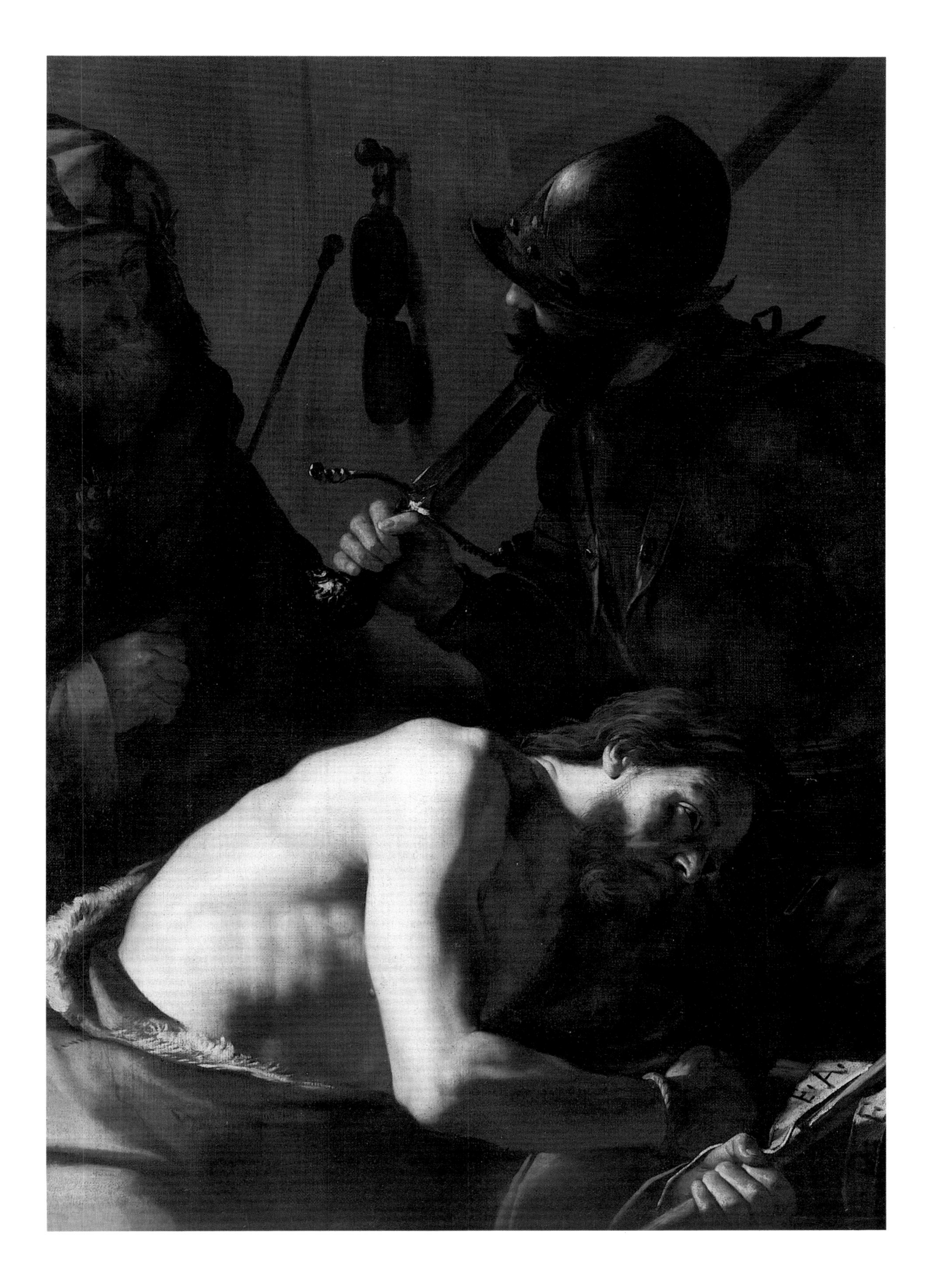

SIR JOSHUA REYNOLDS

PLYMPTON 1723 - 1792 LONDON

Son of a Devon schoolmaster, Reynolds was apprenticed to portraitist Thomas Hudson in London, 1740-43. After modest success between 1743 and 1749, he travelled to Italy to complete his artistic education and was in Rome from 1750 to 1752. Several of his painted caricatures of British and Irish visitors are now in Dublin. He also went to Venice, beginning a lifelong interest in imitating the Venetian colourists. Reynolds returned to London in 1753, and by the 1760s he had become the leading portrait painter of his generation, working in a grand style, with frequent references to mythology, literature and old masters. He ran a large studio and also had his pictures regularly engraved. In 1768, Reynolds was asked to become the first President of the Royal Academy, despite Royal dislike, and was knighted in 1769. His annual Discourses *to students promoted a theory of painting often ignored in his own practice, as with his experiments in paint media. From the 1770s he painted more fancy and subject pictures.*

31 *The Earl of Bellamont,* 1773-74

Oil on canvas, 245 x 162 cm.
NGI Inv. no. 216

This magnificent ceremonial portrait shows Charles Coote, 1st Earl of Bellamont (1738-1800), as a Knight of the Bath. He wears the collar and Star of the Order over a red cloak and satin suit. Coote was MP for County Cavan from 1761 to 1766 and, having put down a minor insurrection in the north of Ireland, was installed at Dublin Castle as a Knight of the Bath in 1764. This chivalric order was founded in 1725 to reward political and military service. Coote succeeded his cousin as Lord Colooney in 1766 and was created Earl of Bellamont in 1767, giving his maiden speech at the Irish House of Lords in French. Contemporaries noted his brilliant conversation but also his vanity and pomposity. The ancestral title was Bellomont but the Earl clearly spelt it with an 'a' as it appears on his banner on the portrait and is now accepted (Penny and Mannings 1986). He fought a duel with former Irish Viceroy Lord Townsend in 1773 over a minor slight and was wounded in the groin. In 1774 he married Lady Emily FitzGerald, daughter of the 1st Duke of Leinster, but they had separated by 1789. His amorous exploits were satirised by *Town and Country Magazine* (1786) which appended engraved portraits of 'The Hibernian Seducer' and one of his victims, a tradesman's daughter who was tricked into a marriage performed by the Earl's servant. His legal son died in 1786 and in his will he acknowledged six illegitimate children by four different mothers. He obtained a baronetcy for his heir.

On 27 October 1773, James Northcote wrote to his brother that 'Sir Joshua is about a very fine whole-length of Lord Bellamont'. The Earl had come for four sittings from late August. For Reynolds, this was a sitter not afraid to show off the more decorative side of his dress, or his shoulder-length hair. No other Knight of the Bath or Garter was ever shown wearing his plumed hat (normally placed on a table) or resting languidly against a sword with feet crossed. The general pose, popularised by Scheemakers' monument to Shakespeare (1741, Westminster Abbey), was used

ARL OF BELLAM

extensively by artists before Reynolds for country house portraits. Here Reynolds gives it a new nobility, though touching it with humour by including an actual coot bird below that on the Earl's banner. The two banners in the distance are of two real military heroes: Major-General Sir William Draper (1721-87) and Rear-Admiral Sir John Moore (1718-79), made Knights of the Bath in 1766 and 1772. The *Public Advertiser* (1774) noted 'The turn of the head and countenance is noble; the figure is graceful, and the drapery magnificent, but for want of harmony hurts the effect of the head'. Doyle (1890) thought it autograph throughout while Armstrong (1898 and 1904) gave the draperies first to Francis Cotes, who by 1773 was an independent rival to Reynolds, then to Peter Toms, who had left Reynolds in the 1760s. Since Reynolds, like Rubens, worked with a team of assistants, their exact contribution can rarely be determined. Giuseppe Marchi was a mainstay for forty years, while from 1771 to 1776, the young painter James Northcote was there. He often modelled for the hands in portraits (*Self-Portrait*, National Portrait Gallery, London) and possibly for the Earl's (see detail). Cleaning has brought out the quality of the satin and lace, depicted in broad confident strokes. The smoothly painted face was painted with vermilion red, while Reynolds used a fugitive red lake or carmine for the cloak and curtain, and probably red lead for the hands, all showing signs of fading.

The Countess of Bellamont sat for a less interesting full-length portrait by Reynolds completed in 1778 (now Luton Hoo), and both were probably hung in the Saloon at the Earl's County Cavan home (renamed Bellamont Forest); they were certainly there by 1837 (Lewis). The present owner, believed to be descended from the Earl, affirms that the earlier plaster wall frames are the correct size for the picture. Their shape is picked up in the eighteenth-century gilt frame, but this was not originally intended for the picture, as restoration has revealed that it was skilfully enlarged by 30cm. in the early nineteenth century.

(ALH)

JACOB VAN RUISDAEL

PROBABLY HAARLEM 1628/9 - 1682 AMSTERDAM OR HAARLEM

Jacob van Ruisdael is generally regarded as the greatest and most versatile landscape painter of the so-called Golden Age of Dutch painting, the seventeenth century. He was probably born in Haarlem, the son of Isaack Jacobsz. van Ruisdael, a frame-maker, picture dealer and painter (no works can be attributed to him with certainty). The precise date of birth is not known but a document dated June 1661 gives his age in that year as thirty-two. He may have studied with his uncle, Salomon van Ruysdael, a leading landscape painter, but he owed more to the influence of the landscapes of Cornelius Vroom. He became a member of the guild at Haarlem in 1648. During the early 1650s, he toured the eastern provinces of the Netherlands along the German border, accompanied by his friend, the artist Nicolaes Berchem. About 1656 or 1657, Ruisdael moved from Haarlem to Amsterdam and remained there for the rest of his life. He died in 1682, and was buried in the grounds of St. Bavo, the great church in his native town of Haarlem. His output was extensive; over 700 works are known.

32 *The Castle of Bentheim,* 1653

Oil on canvas, 110.5 x 44 cm.

Signed: in monogram, and dated 1653 on the rock, left, towards the bottom

NGI Inv. no. 4531 (Beit Collection)

Sutton (1992) has designated this picture, presented to the National Gallery of Ireland in 1987 by Sir Alfred and Lady Beit, as 'the grandest and most ambitious treatment' of the artist's fourteen known paintings of Bentheim Castle. It has long been regarded as one of Ruisdael's best pictures, described in 1835 by John Smith as 'this capital picture ... which deservedly has the reputation of being among the most esteemed works of the master. The composition is of the grandest description, and the execution throughout of the highest excellence; add to which, it has the advantage of the most uncommon purity'. Waagen wrote in 1857 that 'it belongs to the *chefs-d'oeuvre* of the master'. In that year, the picture was one of twenty-two works attributed to Ruisdael which were exhibited at the spectacular Manchester *Art Treasures Exhibition,* a gathering of some 16,000 works loaned from British collections only. Ruisdael's accurately observed, evocative and romantic landscapes appealed to British collectors.

It is important to realise that when Ruisdael painted *The Castle of Bentheim,* in 1653, he was only about twenty-four years of age. He dated many of his paintings between 1646 and 1653, then for some unknown reason he virtually ceased dating his works. Ruisdael's contemporaries acknowledged him as a painter of great promise by allowing him to sign his works before he had reached his twentieth birthday, the age at which painters were permitted to join the Haarlem guild.

Ruisdael never travelled far from his native town and his most ambitious trip was in the early 1650s to the border region between the eastern provinces of the Netherlands and Germany. Among the dated works painted either during these travels, or painted later based on drawings, are his landscapes of the Castle of Bentheim, a small German

town in Westphalia. In these works, Ruisdael exaggerates the site and prominence of the castle in a conscious effort to develop a heroic, monumental, classical style of landscape painting. His forests become more crowded and extensive, his clouds more massive: in brief, he emphasises the awesome power of nature.

Recent scholarship about Dutch seventeenth-century landscape painting has explored the possibility of hidden meanings as found, for example, in Dutch genre painting. Wiegand interpreted Ruisdael's use of Bentheim Castle as an allegory of the Sin of Pride and related it to contemporary emblems and literature. Bruyn disagreed and offered an iconographic explanation for the dramatized view of the castle: 'Bentheim Castle does not appear here for the sake of the topographic motif - which anyway must have been scarcely recognisable to a Dutch audience - but as the castle on the mountain, the eternal city of Zion. Felled trees in the foreground and lacerated or nearly dead trees emphasise the *vanitas* symbolism of the forested area, through which the tiny travellers must move in order to reach their goal'. Walford, in his study of Ruisdael's art, contradicts Bruyn and states that Bentheim Castle was represented primarily as a landmark and that it should be seen as part of the established tradition of representing hilltop castles.

Ruisdael's projection of the castle on to a wooded mountain, the voluminous cloud formations, and the spatial arrangements he creates in the highly worked composition of *The Castle of Bentheim,* while including a marvellous wealth of detail, mark this picture as one of the great landscapes of European painting.

(BPK)

GOTFRIED SCHALCKEN

MADE (DORDECHT) 1634 - 1706 THE HAGUE

Although famous in his lifetime, after his death Gotfried Schalcken's name sank into relative obscurity; it is only in recent times that he has once again been recognised as one of the outstanding painters of the late seventeenth-century Dutch school. His early training (1656-62) was with Samuel Hoogstraten, a follower of Rembrandt, but his prime artistic influence was the Leyden master, Gerard Dou. Schalcken is remarkable not only for his fine style, but also for the variety of his subjects. As well as the candle-lit scenes, for which he is most famous, he painted also genre, historical and religious subjects. His educated background - his father was a minister and a Latin scholar - accounts for the ambitious mythological and allegorical themes which he produced. Commissioned portraits formed a substantial part of his output and he painted at the courts of London (1692-97), for William III, and of Düsseldorf (1703). Schalcken also produced many drawings and engravings. In the late 1690s he settled in The Hague where he remained until his death in 1706. He is the subject of a short story, Schalcken the Painter, *by the Irish writer, Joseph Sheridan Le Fanu.*

33 *Preciosa Recognised,* late 1660s

Oil on panel, rounded at the top, 44.2 x 31.2 cm.

Signed: at bottom, left of centre, *G. Schalcken*

Inscribed: on the paper at the bottom: *het jong ic den* (the young ... [untranslatable])

NGI Inv. no. 476

This small panel, purchased by the Gallery as *The Lost Daughter Restored,* is not only one of Schalcken's masterpieces, but is also an example of the relationship between literature and Dutch painting in the seventeenth century; the scene might be a dramatic moment from a play. The subject is taken from a short story, *La Gitanilla* (The Little Gypsy), the first in Cervantes' collection of twelve *Novelas Ejemplares,* published in Madrid in 1613. Cervantes' work was rapidly disseminated in Holland through translation and adaptation. Spain and the Low Countries had been at war from the latter part of the sixteenth century until finally, in 1648, Philip IV made peace with the Dutch. These contacts, bellicose and peaceful, inevitably led to cultural influences.

The story revolves around the theme of true identity. Constance, the daughter of a noble magistrate, is abducted as a child by a gypsy woman, Majombe. She is given the name Preciosa, which means precious or exquisite, and brought up among gypsies. Later, when Don Juan falls in love with her, she demands that he prove his love by first giving up his noble status and living like her among the gypsies for two years. During that time he is unjustly accused of theft, and while being arrested kills one of the agents of the law and is imprisoned. Preciosa pleads with the magistrate's wife to intercede. Majombe, moved by the lovers' plight, confesses her abduction of the child and reveals that Preciosa is none other than the magistrate's daughter. Schalcken portrays the dramatic moment when Preciosa, dressed in the coarse clothes of a gypsy, draws down her blouse to reveal the moon-shaped mark on her left breast which proves her true identity. Her mother throws up her hands in amazement, while her

father is open-mouthed at this astounding revelation. At the left, in semi-obscurity, the old crone Majombe looks out at the viewer and draws our attention to the evidence which proves her story.

Schalcken heightens the action by focusing attention on Preciosa and her mother; they are centrally placed and strongly lit, while the secondary figures are cast in varying degrees of shadow. In this way he also highlights the delicate skin-tones and blonde hair of the heroine, as well as the satin and brocade finery of the mother. His fine, smooth brushwork, subtle colouring and use of light emphasise Preciosa's female attractiveness. The exquisite still life - pink roses in a marble pot - is symbolic of Preciosa's virginity. Strewn on the ground are the jewels she was wearing at the time of her abduction and the crumpled note announcing the deed. The stick is probably a reference to her itinerant life among the gypsies. In this work Schalcken demonstrates his virtuosity as a great painter in small dimensions, with his impeccable execution and complete mastery of the gradations of light and shade and of scintillating colour. Potterton (1986) and Foucart (Beherman 1988) date the panel to the late 1660s on the basis of style and costume.

(RM)

JAN STEEN

LEIDEN 1625/26 - 1679 LEIDEN

Jan Steen was born at Leiden and was said to be twenty when he enrolled at Leiden University in November 1646. Houbraken states that he was a pupil of Jan van Goyen (whose daughter he married); according to Weyerman his masters were Nicolaus Knupfer at Utrecht, then Adrian van Ostade at Haarlem and finally Jan van Goyen at The Hague. He became a member of the Guild of St. Luke in Leiden in 1648 but by the following year he was living in The Hague. His father, a brewer, leased a brewery for him in Delft between 1654 and 1657 but he does not seem to have spent much time there. From 1656 to 1660 he was certainly living near Leiden, from 1661 to 1670 in Haarlem, and he then returned to Leiden where he remained until his death in 1679. He is not recorded as having had any pupils but his style was much imitated. He was a prolific artist and is best known for his witty genre scenes which often contain moralistic messages.

34 *The Village School,* c.1663-65

Oil on canvas, 110.5 x 80.2 cm.
NGI Inv. no. 226

Jan Steen was a marvellous storyteller and *The Village School* is full of incident. The old schoolmaster holds up a ferule ready to slap a boy who has torn and scribbled on his exercise. The boy presses his hand against his face in anticipation. A girl standing in front of the teacher's table delights in the boy's punishment, but a small boy next to her looks worried that perhaps he might be next. Two more pupils approach the teacher's desk while three others are busy in the background. There are some bottles in a niche on the wall and some books on a shelf, while on the wall itself hang shears, a bottle-type jug and an hourglass. The boxes hanging on the wall to the right are candleboxes, but they were used by children to bring their pencils and other belongings to school. Braun has identified the little girl, the boy being punished and the boy holding his exercise as the painter's three children, Catherina, Cornelis and Johannes. Steen also depicted his children in *Interior of a Schoolroom*, now in the collection of the Marquess of Northampton.

The physical punishment depicted in *The Village School* is mild by seventeenth-century standards. Schoolmasters in the Netherlands were poorly paid, worked very long hours (6.00 am to 7.00 pm during summertime) and had few holidays. Sutton has noted that: 'In some cases, teaching jobs were awarded as social service positions, mere sinecures for those unable to do other work'. It is little wonder that teaching standards were low and teachers were often accused of visiting brothels, failing to provide religious instruction and of excessive drinking. Perhaps the bottle set in the niche implies that the teacher of the village school was a drinker. Potterton suggests that the hourglass is a reminder that children's time must not be wasted. Durantini has related the bookshelf to an emblem by Roemer Visscher in which books are 'Food for the Wild Spirit', a means of taming the unruly, unmannered and unlearned. Both Sutton (1984 Philadelphia) and Braun date the picture to the years 1663 to 1665 when Steen was in Haarlem. The picture has been related to *The Feast of St. Nicolas* in Amsterdam (Rijksmuseum, inv. no A385) which is also dated about 1663-65. Braun lists several copies and imitations.

(BPK)

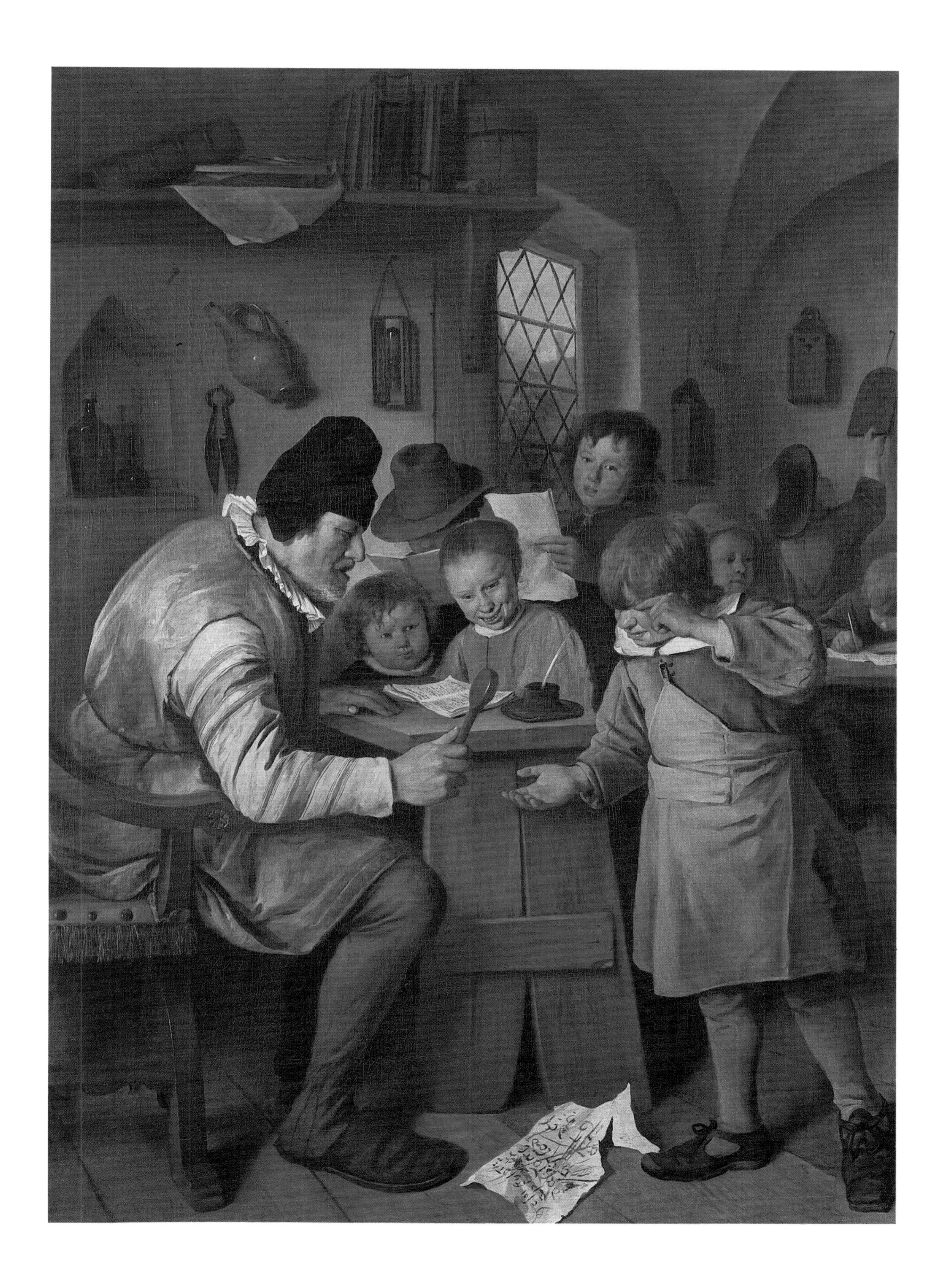

JAN STEEN

35 *The Marriage Feast at Cana,* late 1660s

Oil on panel, 63.5 x 82.5 cm.
Inscribed: right, on the wine barrel, *IHS*
NGI Inv. no. 4534 (Beit Collection)

The story of Jesus Christ's first public miracle, told only in St John's Gospel (Ch. 2, vv. 1-12), is rare in European art. There are few well-known representations of it aside from Tintoretto's version in Santa Maria della Salute, Venice (1561) and the vast picture by Veronese in the Louvre, Paris (1562).

Jan Steen painted the subject at least six times; two of the pictures are dated, 1656 and 1676, and the other four were painted in the late 1660s or early 1670s. Kirschenbaum, van Gelder and Stechow agree that the National Gallery of Ireland's picture, which was probably painted on private commission, can be dated to the late 1660s. This picture has long been praised for its quality and its tremendous detail but it has also been criticised for its undignified approach to a sacred subject. Smith remarked: 'The total incapacity of Jan Steen to render the necessary dignity of character and expression to his figures, so indispensable in an historical subject, is no less evident in this picture than in every other example of a similar kind; in all other respects the talents and genius of the artist are strikingly evinced'. Schmidt-Degener suggested that the inscription I.H.S. applied not just to the artist's name, Jan Havicks Steen, but also to the so-called 'sacred letters of Constantine', *In Hoc Signo (vinces)* (in this sign thou shalt conquer), thus implying that the picture was about the theme of drunkenness. Watson described the painting as extraordinary and impressive, but the religious theme is 'perhaps treated too curiously in the Dutch genre style to appeal greatly to the modern taste'.

Stechow has interpreted Steen's pictures of the Cana miracle as didactic works about the real presence of Christ in the Catholic Eucharist. He points out that the key figure in Steen's picture is the young man in the right foreground who is looking towards the figure of Christ, and is holding his right hand against his heart while pointing with his left hand towards the fountain (the water of life). It is this young man who filled the pitchers with water and he therefore recognises a miracle when Christ turns the water into wine.

It is thought that Steen was inspired by theatrical stage sets in the compositions for his paintings of the marriage feast at Cana. There is a tradition that the Rederijkers (Rhetoricians) performed masques of the Cana miracle at wedding feasts in seventeenth-century Holland. It is likely that Steen also owed a debt to Raphael's composition in *The School of Athens* (Vatican) with which he may have been familiar from a print or drawing.

(BPK)

BERNARDO STROZZI

GENOA 1581 - 1644 VENICE

Trained as a painter and educated for the priesthood in the Capuchin order, Strozzi was allowed to leave the order, but remain a priest, to take care of his mother. He painted extensively in and around Genoa. When his mother died in 1630 there was some question of his returning to his friary; apparently he chose to join the Canons Regular of the Lateran, and it was about this time that he transferred to Venice. He remained known, however, as 'il prete genovese' *(the Genoese priest).*

36 *Spring and Summer,* c.1640

Oil on canvas, 72 x 128 cm.
NGI Inv. no. 856

Two half-length female figures hold the attributes of their respective seasons; on the left is Summer, holding a sack of fruit with sprigs of corn in her hair; on the right is Spring, holding flowers in both hands, her hair decorated with more flowers. One should note that in Italy both fruit and corn ripen in summer, much earlier than in the western extremities of Europe, such as England and Ireland. The attribution to Strozzi is quite secure. The catalogue of the 1959 exhibition at Venice says that it belongs to the artist's last phase, while Potterton, in the catalogue of the 1979 exhibition in London, places it at the end of the 1630s. By this time Strozzi had fully absorbed all the lessons of Venetian colouring and light. Moreover, there is an exceptionally rich use of impasto. Potterton correctly links it stylistically to *The Personification of Fame* in the National Gallery, London.

One would suppose that this painting had a pendant depicting Autumn and Winter, but if such ever existed it has not yet come to light. As pendants they would have made splendid overdoors. The painting was bought in Rome by the 6th Viscount Powerscourt. His son, in a detailed account of Powerscourt (Powerscourt 1903), describes the precise location of *Spring and Summer* as hanging in the Drawing Room over the door leading into the Saloon. No other Strozzi is mentioned as being in the Drawing Room, or elsewhere in the house, so one must presume that only one was bought.

Mortari (1966) relates a drawing of a female head in the Suida Manning Collection, New York, to the small *Annunciation* painting in the Museum of Fine Arts, Budapest; the drawing shows a slightly down-turned head, whereas the Virgin's head in the Budapest painting is upturned. The drawing is in fact much closer to the head of Summer here (as suggested by Potterton in the catalogue of the 1979 exhibition), with its serious countenance. However, no strict connection can really be claimed, because the face of Summer is facing to the right while that in the drawing is facing to the left.

(MW)

GIOVANNI BATTISTA TIEPOLO

VENICE 1696 - 1770 MADRID

A painter of light, airy, elegant compositions in fresco and in oil, Tiepolo is arguably the greatest painter of the Rococo style. He was influenced by Veronese among the old masters and by Sebastiano Ricci and Piazetta among his contemporaries. Tiepolo worked widely in Italy and in 1750 he travelled to Würtsburg with his sons, Giandomenico and Lorenzo, to decorate the Residence of the Prince-Bishop. In 1755, after his return to Venice, he was elected president of the Venetian Academy. In 1762, accompanied by his sons and assistants, he went to Madrid at the invitation of Charles III, and remained there until his death in 1770.

37 *Allegory of the Immaculate Conception,* c.1769

Oil on paper, laid on canvas, 58.7 x 45 cm.
NGI Inv. no. 353

In this unusual representation of the Immaculate Conception, God the Father, surrounded by angels, appears to the Virgin, while the Holy Spirit in the form of a dove hovers above. The Virgin kneels to receive God's blessing and to submit to her role in mankind's Redemption. The traditional attributes of the Virgin Mary's Immaculate Conception - that she was conceived without the stain of original sin - are represented by the halo of stars and the crescent moon (*Apocalypse* Ch. 12, v. 1). The serpent crawling on the terrestrial globe holds in its mouth an apple, the traditional image of the fruit of the Tree of Paradise which Adam was forbidden to touch (*Genesis* Ch. 2, vv. 15-17). The mirror, symbol of the Virgin's purity and virtue, is held by an angel in a threatening manner against the serpent, who recoils from it. The palm tree, symbol of victory and celebration, shown here as fallen, may represent the fall of man. The obelisk, which carries an indecipherable inscription, possibly in Hebrew, may be a reference to the Tower of David, a medieval title for the Virgin. The concept of the obelisk as symbolic of honour or glory makes it appropriate here, as the Virgin is sometimes referred to as the Glory of Jerusalem.

This small work on paper is a particularly fine example of Tiepolo's mastery of the oil sketch. The vitality of the draughtsmanship, the richness of the colouring and the manner in which the main passages are highly finished, while other areas are thinly sketched, are characteristic of his *modelli.* The expression of spiritual intensity and devotion is indicative of his last years. There is no record of a canvas for which the Dublin picture might have been a *modello.* However, Catherine Whistler and Michael Levey have, independently, surmised that it represents Tiepolo's first thoughts for the fresco decoration of the dome of the collegiate church of San Ildefonso at La Granja, a commission he was given by Charles III in 1769. Tiepolo died in 1770 before he could begin the fresco.

The provenance of the Dublin painting has proved difficult to trace. However, Whistler convincingly identifies it with the late *modello* mentioned by the Venetian dealer Pietro Edwards in a letter to Antonio Canova in 1804. Edwards described an unusual Dantesque version of the Immaculate Conception which he deemed worthy of inclusion in Canova's collection.

(RM)

TIZIANO VECELLIO, CALLED TITIAN

PIEVE DI CADORE c.1488/90 - 1576 VENICE

Titian, a son of Gregorio Vecellio, notary, was born in the village of Pieve di Cadore, north of Venice. When still very young, he was apprenticed with Sebastiano Zuccato in Venice. He then entered the studio of Gentile Bellini, where he surely met Giovanni Bellini, the most important influence for his early development. By 1508 Titian had already established a reputation for himself and was commissioned, along with Giorgione, to decorate the Fondaco dei Tedeschi on the Grand Canal. In 1515 he began to paint the altarpiece for the great Franciscan church of I Frari, arguably the first monumental High Renaissance work to be created in Venice. His reputation firmly established, Titian now won commissions from a host of illustrious patrons throughout Europe, including the Pope and the Emperor. In his late forties, following a brief involvement with Mannerism, he developed a mature manner which became increasingly personal and which produced a sequence of masterpieces which today rank among the most profound achievements of Western culture.

38 *Ecce Homo,* late 1550s

Oil on canvas, 72 x 55 cm.
NGI Inv. no. 75

The image of the tortured Christ, beaten and crowned with thorns, is taken from the Vulgate version of the Bible (*John* Ch.19, vv.4-6). Its iconographic origins derive from images of the Man of Sorrows, a subject popular with medieval artists, and images of the veil of St. Veronica (the *Sudarium*); this cloth, according to legend, retained the image of Christ's bloodstained features when Veronica wiped his face on the road to Calvary. Titian painted many versions of this particular subject, a number of them accompanied by complementary images of the Virgin as *Mater Dolorosa* (Mother of Sorrows), a formula made popular by the Northern masters. Documentary evidence (Wethey 1972) indicates that Titian's first representation of the *Ecce Homo* subject was delivered to the Emperor Charles V at Augsburg in 1548. The Emperor had a strong attachment to devotional images of the suffering Christ painted by artists such as the followers of Roger van der Weyden, and had requested Titian to paint a similar work. He later commissioned a painting of the *Mater Dolorosa* to be placed alongside the *Ecce Homo* to form a diptych. Charles V took both paintings with him when he retired to the monastery at Yuste in 1557.

Titian's authorship of this painting has not always been accepted. In 1914, Armstrong attributed it to Matteo Cerezo. However, the cleaning of the picture in 1954, which removed overpainting to the face and beard, revealed the masterly handling of the subject and brought clearly to light the *pentimenti* in the position of the reed and the rope tied around Christ's wrists. In the following year St. John Gore (1955) published the restored canvas as the work of Titian. MacGreevy, in his catalogue of the Italian paintings in the collection (1956), reaffirmed the attribution, citing Berenson, Wilde and Lionello Venturi. Subsequent writers have supported the attribution to Titian, noting its relationship to the Ancona altarpiece of 1558, exemplifying Titian's late style in which, as Vasari states, the images are painted roughly and impressionistically, being designed to be viewed from a distance.

(RK)

CORNELIS TROOST

AMSTERDAM 1696 - 1750 AMSTERDAM

Cornelis Troost, like his English contemporary William Hogarth (1697-1764), painted conversation pieces. Influenced by French models, he was one of the painters who put new life into this genre, which had been declining in Holland from the beginning of the eighteenth century. The son of a goldsmith, he was a pupil of Arnold Booner, then the most sought-after painter in Amsterdam. Troost moved in theatrical and musical circles, marrying Susanna Maria van Duyn, the daughter of an actress and singer, in Zwolle in 1720. He painted stage sets and scenes from theatrical performances; he himself is recorded as an actor in Amsterdam in 1718 and again in the 1720s. Troost was as skilled a draughtsman as he was a painter in oils, and he particularly excelled when working in pastel.

39 *Jeronimus Tonneman and his son Jeronimus: The Dilettanti,* 1736

Oil on panel, 68 x 58 cm.
Signed and dated: on the skirting board beneath the statue, *C. Troost 1736*
NGI Inv. no. 497

In this double portrait Troost portrays one of his most important sitters, Jeronimus Tonneman the elder (1687-1750), and his son Jeronimus. Their identities have been established by a comparison with a miniature portrait of Jeronimus Tonneman by Henriette Wolters-van Pee in an Amsterdam private collection. Tonneman owned the artist's self-portrait and also his major conversation-piece, *The Spendthrift,* both now in the Rijksmuseum, Amsterdam. The French-style interior in which the men are seated is not real, but idealised. The younger Tonneman is playing a flute and on the table a copy of Van Mander's *Het Schilder-boeck,* the most important source on the lives of the early Dutch painters, is used as a prop for his music. The father's seated pose is similar to *The Musician* (Rijksmuseum), which was also painted by Troost in 1736.

In this small masterpiece the play of light and shadow is keenly observed and the various textures are conveyed with smooth yet lively brushstrokes. Troost uses the contrast between the singing scarlet tones of the younger Tonneman's apparel, and the sombre tones of his father's, to great effect. The turned-back corner of the Turkey carpet eloquently disturbs the formality of the room and introduces a sense of temporality which is reinforced by the stucco relief on the background wall of *Time Revealing Truth and Banishing Slander.* The roundel above the chimneypiece shows *Mercury Killing Argus.* According to Ovid, Mercury did this by first lulling Argus to sleep with piped music; Van Mander links the episode with the disastrous effects of the pursuit of wealth and idle fame, resulting in the destruction of justice, reason and virtue. The plaster saint in the niche is modelled on Duquesnoy's *St. Susanna,* and its inclusion may have been more for reasons of decoration - as a studio prop - than symbolism, for Troost included the statue in another composition, *Blind Man's Buff.*

It has been suggested that the patron wished to be portrayed, not only as a patron of art and music, but also as someone who was aware of the vanity of worldly pursuits. It is a grim irony that the year after the picture was painted Jeronimus the younger stabbed his mistress, who had borne him a child, and fled to the East Indies.

(RM)

DIEGO DE SILVA VELÁZQUEZ

SEVILLE 1599 - 1660 MADRID

Velázquez, one of the great masters of European art, was born in Seville in 1599, son of Juan Rodríguez de Silva and Jerónima Velázquez. In 1611 he entered the studio of Francisco Pacheco, whose daughter he married in 1618. Velázquez's early work is strongly naturalistic and includes a series of kitchen or tavern scenes (bodegones), *religious subjects and portraits. In 1622 he made his first visit to Madrid and the following year returned to that city where he was soon to become a court painter, immortalising Philip IV, his family and entourage. The study of the royal collections and his friendship with Rubens influenced his development, and two visits to Italy, in 1629-31 and 1649-51, transformed his style. His mature work is very different from the chiaroscuro approach of his early style. His free brushwork, light colouring and masterly ability to create an atmosphere around his figures made him a source of inspiration for later generations of painters, particularly the Impressionists. Velázquez held several official offices at court, including that of Palace Chamberlain. In 1659 he was made a Knight of Santiago, a singular honour for an artist.*

40 *Kitchen Maid with the Supper at Emmaus,* c.1618-19

Oil on canvas, 55 x 118 cm.
NGI Inv. no. 4538 (Beit Collection)

In this early painting by Velázquez a Moorish kitchen maid is shown, half-length, leaning over a table on which kitchen utensils are arranged. She pauses in her work as though aware of the scene visible through a hatch at the left, the Supper at Emmaus (*Luke* Ch. 24, v. 28). St. Luke tells how two of the disciples on the day of the Resurrection went to the village of Emmaus. On the way they met Jesus, whom they did not recognise and who walked with them. When they reached Emmaus they invited him to join them for supper at an inn. 'And it came to pass, as he sat at meat with them, he took bread, and blessed it, and brake, and gave to them. And their eyes were opened, and they knew him; and he vanished out of their sight.'

In sixteenth- and seventeenth-century Spain, the term *bodegón* was applied to paintings which combined still-life and *genre* in a kitchen or tavern setting. Francisco Pacheco (1564-1654), painter, theorist and father-in-law of Velázquez, held that the *bodegón* painter was successful according to the extent of his ability to imitate nature. In his treatise on painting, *Arte de la Pintura,* he asks the rhetorical question, 'Should we not value *bodegones*? But of course - if they are painted as my son-in-law painted them, who surpasses all others in this *genre* and merits the greatest esteem.' The inclusion of a religious scene would have raised the *bodegón* to a higher level and increased its value.

Using a restricted palette of ochres, earth colours and white, characteristic of his early work, Velázquez conveys the surface textures of the glazed and burnished vessels. The glazed pottery jugs and dishes, the mortar and pestle and the head of garlic are familiar objects in his *bodegones,* which are revolutionary in their direct confrontation with nature. The light falling from the left highlights the white cap, forehead and cheek of the kitchen maid, whose arrested presence presides over the masterly still-life. The composition achieves a balance between the figure and the still-life, neither

of which dominates. The figures in the background are painted in a nervous sketchy manner which is at variance with the calm volumetric treatment of the foreground. As the canvas has been cut down on the left, the arm only of the second disciple is visible. This scene was uncovered in 1933 during cleaning.

The device of 'a picture within a picture' was common in late sixteenth- and seventeenth-century painting. Kitchen scenes with a religious subject in the background were popular in sixteenth-century Flemish painting; Velázquez would have seen such paintings, or engravings of them. The only other known *bodegón* with a religious scene by Velázquez, *Kitchen Scene with Christ in the House of Martha and Mary* in the National Gallery, London, bears the date 1618. It shows a kitchen maid and an old woman with an arrangement of fish and utensils on a table, and in the background a scene representing Christ in the house of Martha and Mary. These paintings appear to have a didactic purpose. In the Dublin painting, the girl seems to be aware that something of moment is taking place; the miraculous occurrence amidst the humdrum, everyday chores of life. There may be a further significance in the fact that the maid is a Moor. There were many slaves in Seville in the early seventeenth century working as domestic servants, some of whom converted to Christianity. The painting would seem to imply that even for this lowly slave there is the possibility of salvation.

A third painting, *Two Young Men at Table* (The Wellington Museum, Apsley House), resembles the Dublin painting in style and format, and another dated *bodegón* by Velázquez is the *Old Woman Cooking Eggs,* 1618 (National Gallery of Scotland), in which similar kitchen objects are used. The Dublin *bodegón* belongs to the above-mentioned group of early works and may be dated c.1618-19. There is a replica, without the background scene, in the Art Institute of Chicago.

(RM)

SIMON VOUET

PARIS 1590 - 1649 PARIS

The son of an obscure painter, Laurent Vouet, and grandson of Nicolas Vouet, Falconer to the King in Chamagne, Simon was born in Paris on 8 January 1590. At fourteen he went to England, at twenty-one to Constantinople (1611-12), and from there to Venice (1612-13), arriving in Rome probably at the beginning of 1614. Between 1620 and 1621 he was in Genoa, where he worked for the Doria family. In 1624, he was elected president of the Accademia di San Luca - the first foreigner to be accorded this honour. He was one of the most celebrated artists in Rome when he was recalled to Paris in 1627 as Premier Peintre du Roi, *bringing with him a fully developed Baroque style, and moreover the organisational ability to co-ordinate the subsequent flow of commissions for altarpieces and large-scale decorative cycles. He established a large studio, where many great painters of the next generation were trained.*

41 *The Four Seasons,* c.1644-45

Oil on canvas, 113 cm. in diameter
NGI Inv. no. 1982

Vouet, at ease whether painting religious or profane subjects, delighted in the portrayal of the human body; lusty, healthy figures people his canvases. Here, Flora (Spring, synonymous with Venus), identified by the wreath of flowers and the crown she is holding, exchanges an amorous look with Adonis (Winter), clad as a hunter. They are watched by Ceres (Summer) who carries a sickle and ears of corn while, below, the infant Bacchus (Autumn) carrying grapes is frightened by the dog.

Vouet's interpretation of the four seasons is unprecedented. He presents the moment of union between Venus and Adonis. The theme is expanded in the inscription on Dorigny's engraving of 1645: 'What nature denies, a picture has been able to show / The union of sluggish cold with fruits and wreath of flowers'. In Greek mythology Adonis, born of a myrrh tree, spent one part of the year underground with the goddess Persephone, and the other part with Aphrodite on earth. Traditionally associated with the generative forces in Nature, it was by accident that he came to personify Winter. It is probable that Vouet drew on Ripa's *Iconologia* as his source, where under the heading *Inverno* Ripa writes: 'One should paint winter as a beautiful young Adonis in the guise of a hunter...'

A painting of the same subject in Glasgow, regarded by Crelly (1981) as an earlier version of *The Four Seasons,* is now, however, attributed to Dorigny (Thuillier 1990). The Dublin picture is compositionally more refined, recalling fifteenth-century Tuscan tondos. The curved diagonal form of Adonis dominates the composition, while the angle of each head creates a circular movement echoing the shape of the canvas. The arm movements, Ceres' head-dress, and the wreaths worn and held by Venus and the infant Bacchus continue this theme of curves and arcs throughout the picture. The flat pale blue background throws the figures into relief; and the pale, rather cool colours emphasise the gay, decorative quality of the tondo. It can be dated c.1644-45.

(FC)

JAN BAPTIST WEENIX

AMSTERDAM 1621 - c.1660-61 HUIS TER MEY, NEAR UTRECHT

The early eighteenth-century art historian and painter, Arnold Houbraken, states that Jan Baptist Weenix was born in Amsterdam in 1621 and was a pupil of Jan Micker in Amsterdam, of Abraham Bloemart in Utrecht and finally of Nicolaes Moeyart in Amsterdam. Aged eighteen, he married a daughter of the landscape painter, Gillis d'Hondecoeter, grandfather of Melchior d'Hondecoeter. He made a will in Amsterdam in 1642 before setting out to study in Italy. He spent his time there mainly in Rome where he worked for Cardinal Giovanni Battista Pamphili (later Pope Innocent X). By June 1647 he had returned to Amsterdam but had settled in Utrecht by 1649. He signed himself Johannes Weeninckс *or* Weenincx *until 1643, but after his years in Italy he invariably signed his pictures* Gio(vanni) Batt(ist)a Weenix. *Houbraken says that Weenix died at his country house, Huis ter Mey, near Utrecht, at the age of thirty-nine. He was a prolific artist and his output includes idealised Italianate landscapes and seaports, still life with dead game, and some portraits. His son, Jan Weenix, was also a painter.*

42 *The Sleeping Shepherdess*, c.1656-58

Oil on canvas, 72.5 x 61.1 cm.
Signed: on the architrave above the left-hand column, *Gio : Batta Weenix.*
NGI Inv. no. 511

This charming picture shows a girl asleep before a classical ruin with a dog standing alert beside her. Although the picture is a setpiece and the landscape is idealised, a ruin somewhere in Italy, the details are wonderfully observed. An amusing wide flat hat shades the sleeping shepherdess, gentle sunlight falls on the flesh of her neck, the hairs on the guard dog's legs and on its tail are erect, travellers sit drinking at a table in the background, on the horizon there are ships at sea.

In 1808 the then owner of the picture, François-Xavier de Burtin, described it as 'one of the best paintings by this great artist'. In 1878, Fétis called it 'one of the principal ornaments of the Gallery of the Duke of Brunswick-Wolfenbuttel at Salzthalum'. Ginnings suggests a date of 1656-58 for the picture. It is of interest that Weenix's *Rest on the Flight into Egypt* (c.1647-50), now in the Philadelphia Museum of Art (inv. no. E1984-1-1), was also in Salzthalum and was later owned by de Burtin. It shows a Madonna and child with an obedient dog. This dog motif was a symbol for the willingness to learn in the emblematic literature of Jacob Cats and others. It may also symbolise Christian discipline.

The artist's son, Jan Weenix, painted a similarly composed picture now in Munich (Alte Pinakothek, inv. no. 246) and Schloss has pointed out that a moral is intended: the girl is a spinner who is neglecting her work through sleep and idleness. Potterton (1986) stated that no moral is intended in the Dublin picture in which he considers 'the artist has been primarily concerned to convey the appearance and atmosphere of Italy'. Recent scholarship by Nanette Salomon on images of sleep in Dutch genre painting has focused attention on the condemnation of heavy slumber by Dutch moralists and, consequently, it is possible that *The Sleeping Shepherdess* contains a metaphorical message.

(BPK)

FRANCIS WHEATLEY

LONDON 1747 - 1801 LONDON

Son of a master tailor, Wheatley had little formal training, but took up small full-length portraits and conversation pieces modelled on Zoffany. Large debts, and an affair with Elizabeth, the wife of fellow artist John Gresse, led him to flee with her to Dublin in 1779, where she was passed off as his own wife. His Irish works are amongst his finest, with congenial individual patrons and enlarged conversation piece groups. He also painted watercolour landscapes and genre scenes. Returning to London in 1783, he continued to exhibit Irish subjects but gave up portraiture for sentimental, and often moralising, genre subjects. Wheatley was elected an Associate of the Royal Academy in 1790 and Member in 1791.

43 *The Marquess and Marchioness of Antrim,* 1782

Oil on canvas, 99.7 x 128.3 cm.
Signed and dated: lower right on rock, *F Wheatley px 1782*
NGI Inv. no. 4339

Randal William McDonnell, 6th Earl of Antrim (1749-91) and his wife Letitia (d. 1801) are depicted riding in their yellow phaeton against their estate, Glenarm, County Antrim, while two grooms in buff uniforms follow them on horseback. He was created a Marquess in 1789, hence the title of the picture. On his coat, he proudly displays the Star of the Order of the Bath. His wife was the daughter of the 1st Viscount Mountmorres and they married in 1774, when she was already the widow of the Hon. Arthur Trevor. She wears a riding habit and an elaborate hat with feathers in the latest style. As they had no male heir, a special patent was granted in 1785 transferring the Earldom to their daughters.

Wheatley developed the composition from an earlier group of *Lord Carlisle in the Phoenix Park with his Family* (1781, Castle Howard). He painted his sitters in Dublin, but must have been given a view of the house, situated on the coast north of Belfast, as the general terrain is accurate, as in a late eighteenth-century view (Ulster Museum, Belfast). The mid-eighteenth-century three-storey house with curving wings seen here was later rebuilt in Elizabethan style. Beyond in the village are the spires of St Peter's church and the courthouse (now demolished). Though artificial, the landscape colouring is an attractive grey-green, with fine passages in the silver birch and the magnificent chestnut horses. The format of actual, or implied, portraits of landowners in a carriage against their country house was first popularised in England by Jan Siberechts in the seventeenth century.

(ALH)

RANDAL Wm 2nd MARQUIS of ANTRIM
and His Wife LETITIA

FRANCISCO DE ZURBARÁN

FUENTE DE CANTOS (BADAJOZ) 1598 - 1664 MADRID

In 1614 Zurbarán began a three-year apprenticeship in Seville with Pedro Díaz de Villanueva, a painter about whom we know nothing and none of whose work has survived. During these formative years Velázquez was also in Seville and his naturalistic style influenced the young Zurbarán. In 1617 Zurbarán moved to Llerena (Badajoz) where he married María Páez Jiménez, the first of three wives. In 1629 he settled in Seville at the invitation of the town council and became the painter par excellence *of the religious orders - Carthusians, Dominicans, Mercedarians, Jesuits, Franciscans and Hieronymites - from whom he received large commissions. In 1634 he made a trip to Madrid to paint a series of canvases for the Salon de los Reinos in the Buen Retiro palace. Zurbarán had a busy workshop which exported paintings to the Spanish provinces in America. From 1650 his fortunes declined, partly due to the rising reputation of Murillo in Seville. This probably brought about his move to Madrid, where he is documented in December 1658 as a witness on behalf of Velázquez before the tribunal investigating the latter's claims to nobility. He died in Madrid on 27 August 1664, at the age of sixty-six.*

44 *The Immaculate Conception,* early 1660s

Oil on canvas, 166 x 108.5 cm.
NGI Inv. no. 273

The Virgin of the Immaculate Conception is shown as a young girl, in white dress and blue mantle and with hands folded across her breast. She stands upon a full moon, clothed by the sun and crowned by stars, as the woman of the Apocalypse described by St. John (*Revelation* Ch. 12, v. 1). Set in a lush Sevillian landscape with a view of the city are her symbols - the cypress (like a cypress tree on Mount Sion), palm (thy stature is like a palm-tree), temple (temple of the Holy Ghost and temple of David), tower (Tower of David and Tower of Ivory), well (well of living waters), fountain (a garden enclosed, a fountain sealed), star (*stella maris*), gate (*porta caeli*). Countless representations of the Immaculate Conception were painted in Spain in the seventeenth century, though it was not officially proclaimed dogma until 1854.

This representation closely follows the views of Francisco Pacheco, adviser on religious art to the Holy Office of the Inquisition, as to how the subject should be painted. However, the presence of the two allegorical figures is unusual and possibly unique, and suggests that this was a commissioned work, possibly for a cleric. The figure on the left, whose eyes are concealed by the Virgin's mantle, represents Faith and the figure on the right, holding an anchor, represents Hope. Michael Wynne has suggested that the Virgin in this context represents the third theological virtue, Charity. The landscape setting for the subject is part of a Sevillian tradition established in the early part of the seventeenth century; the *Virgin of the Immaculate Conception,* c.1618, by Velázquez (National Gallery, London) and the *Virgin of the Immaculate Conception with Miguel Cid,* 1621, by Pacheco (Seville Cathedral), are notable examples. Among Zurbarán's own oeuvre, the composition and landscape also relate to the *Immaculate Conception with Two Young Noblemen,* 1632, in the Museo de Arte de Cataluña, Barcelona.

This painting was not widely known nor accepted as an authentic Zurbarán until traces of a signature were discovered during cleaning in 1981. The signature had been effaced some time prior to 1886, possibly with a view to passing the picture off as by Murillo, whose work was then fetching high prices. It was purchased by the Gallery as by Valdés Leal and remained catalogued as such until 1928 when the attribution was changed to Zurbarán. In 1922 Mayer had written that it was definitely not by Valdés Leal, but a late work by Zurbarán – post 1640: 'Like all work of the artist's last period it shows distinct traces of Murillo's influence which has destroyed Zurbarán's original harsh and austere style and substitutes for it a gentle and soft manner. The Dublin picture is very characteristic of this'. Soria rejected Mayer's attribution in 1958 (letter, NGI archive). María Luisa Caturla, after carrying out a thorough examination of the picture in 1959, pronounced it to be not only authentic, but very important as an example of Zurbarán's late phase, perhaps his last year.

There are thirteen known versions of this subject by Zurbarán. The pose of the Virgin in the Dublin painting resembles that in the Valdés collection, Bilbao, while the curve of the body, the bow and the positioning of the *cartellino* bearing the signature are similar to the *Immaculate Conception* at Bordeaux. The influence of his rival, Murillo, who eclipsed him towards the end of his career, can be seen in the softening of his austere style, particularly in the vaporous treatment of the cherubim and the clouds into which they subtly merge. It was probably painted in Madrid in the very last years of his life and shows that Zurbarán's creative powers had not diminished.

(RM)

DOCUMENTATION

HENDRICK AVERCAMP

Scene on the Ice, c.1620

Provenance: T. Humphry Ward, by whom presented, 1900.

NGI Catalogues: Potterton 1981, p. 3. Potterton 1986, pp. 3-4.

Selected References: Welcker 1933, no. S45, p. 207. Welcker 1979, no. S45, p. 210. 1980 Mauritshuis, p. 4, no. 785. 1982 Amsterdam/Zwolle, p. 27, fig. 9. Blankert 1982, pp. 604-15. 1986 Paris, pp. 128-29 (under no. 5). 1987 Amsterdam, pp. 258-59.

POMPEO GIROLAMO BATONI

Joseph Leeson, afterwards 1st Earl of Milltown, 1744

Provenance: Commissioned from the artist by the sitter; the Leeson family, Earls of Milltown; Milltown Gift 1902.

Exhibitions: 1982 Kenwood, no. 1.

NGI Catalogues: Potterton 1981, p. 7. Wynne 1986, pp. 5-6.

Selected References: Neale 1826, n.p. Milltown 1863, p. 7. Georgian Soc. Records 1913, pp. 68-71. Steegman 1946, pp. 55 ff. Wynne 1974, pp. 104 ff. Russell 1982, p. 94. Clark 1985, pp. 233-34, no. 87; Cat. nos. 148, 149.

BERNARDO BELLOTTO

Dresden from the Right Bank of the Elbe above the Augustus Bridge, c.1750

Provenance: M.B. Naryschkin Collection, at whose sale, Paris, 5 April 1883, lot 2, bought for £379 with below.

Exhibitions: 1911 London, no. 21. 1954-55 London, no. 302. 1985 London, no. 8. 1990 Verona, no. 43.

NGI Catalogues: Potterton 1981, p. 9. Wynne 1986, pp.11-12.

Selected References: Hempel 1965, pp. 196-98. Kozakiewicz 1972, p. 115, no. 144. Gemäldegalerie 1979, p. 103, no. 606. Garstang 1987, p. 152.

BERNARDO BELLOTTO

Dresden from the Right Bank of the Elbe below the Augustus Bridge, c.1750

Provenance: M.B. Naryschkin Collection, at whose sale, Paris, 5 April 1883, lot 2, bought for £379 with above.

Exhibitions: 1911 London, no. 17. 1985 London, no. 9.

NGI Catalogues: Potterton 1981, p. 9. Wynne 1986, p. 12.

Selected References: Kozakiewicz 1972, p. 121, no. 150. Garstang 1987, p. 152. 1990 Verona, pp. 144-47.

GIOVANNI BENEDETTO CASTIGLIONE

The Shepherdess Spako with the Infant Cyrus, 1650s

Provenance: The Dukes of Mantua; the 9th Earl of Lincoln (subsequently 2nd Duke of Newcastle-under-Lyme) by 1765; by descent to the Earl of Lincoln (heir to the 8th Duke of Newcastle-under-Lyme), by whom consigned for sale at Christie's, 4 June 1937, lot 19, where bought for £378.

Exhibitions: 1857 Manchester, no. 834. 1985 London, no. 6.

NGI Catalogues: Potterton 1981, p. 22. Wynne 1986, pp. 18-20.

Selected References: Delogu 1928, pl. 18. Cappelli 1930, pp. 317ff. Blunt 1954, p. 40, no. 183 and p. 33, fig. 15. Torriti 1967, p. 28, fig. 20; p. 30, fig. 21; p. 300, n. 12. Percy 1971, p. 126. Meroni 1971, p. 108, no. 1. Whistler 1987, p. 67.

JEAN~SIMÉON CHARDIN

Card Tricks (Les Tours de Cartes), c.1735

Provenance: (?) Giroux sale, Monday, 10 Feb. 1851, no. 39; (?) coll. Laurent Laperlier; coll. Moitessier, 1871; Vicomtesse de Bondy Sale, 20-21 May 1898, no. 183; purchased from Colnaghi's, London, 1898 for £750.

Exhibitions: (?) 1739 Paris. 1918 London, no. 9. 1968 London, no. 132.

NGI Catalogues: Potterton 1981, p. 23.

Selected References: Bocher 1876, p. 102. Pilon 1909, pp. 49, 73. Furst 1911, p. 133. Bodkin 1925, p. 94. Pascal and Gaucheron 1931, p. 72. de Ridder 1932, pp. ii, 68, pl. LXIII. Wildenstein 1933, no. 181; 1963 ed., no. 155; 1969 ed. revised and enlarged by D. Wildenstein 1969, no. 155. Denvir 1950, p. 30. Rosenberg 1983a, no. 95. Rosenberg 1983b, pp. 23, 25, 26, 60 (n. 24), 64 (n. 25).

CLAUDE LORRAIN

Juno Confiding Io to the Care of Argus, 1660

Provenance: Gaillard de Gagny sale, Remy, Paris, 29 March 1762, lot 32. Duc de Choiseul sale, Boileau, (?) Paris, 6 April 1772, lot 124; Louis-François de Bourbon, Prince de Conti sale, Remy, Paris, 8 April 1777, lot 554, bt. Langlier; Walshe Porter sale, Christie's, London, 23 March 1803, lot 44, 700 guineas, bt. Major Price; R. Heathcote sale, Phillips, London, 6 April 1805, lot 96, bt. Charles Hanbury Tracey (later Lord Sudley, 1838); thence by descent; anonymous (Lord Sudley) sale, Christie's, London, 27 May 1882, lot 94, bt. Lesser for A. Coats; his sale, Christie's, London, 3 May 1914, lot 124, bt. Sir Hugh Lane by whom bequeathed, 1915, and received in the Gallery (Lane Bequest), 1918.

Exhibitions: 1821 London, no. 43. 1832 London, no. 43. 1883 Edinburgh, no. 458. 1918 Dublin, no. 37. 1925 Paris, no. 126. 1962 Bologna, no. 101. 1964 Newcastle-upon-Tyne, no. 20. 1964 London, no. 31. 1985 Dublin, no. 15.

NGI Catalogues: Potterton 1981, p. 24.

Selected References: Dunker and Maillet 1771, pl. 110. Smith 1837, part 8, p. 273, no. 149. Pattison 1884, p. 219. Courthion 1932, pl. 36. Roethlisberger 1960, pp. 209-24. Kitson 1962 exh. note. Roethlisberger 1968, vol. I, p. 311, no. 829, vol. II, fig 829. White 1968, pp. 36, 70, pl. 14. Pigler 1974, vol. 1, p. 129. Roethlisberger 1977, no. 219. Kitson 1978, p. 145, under no. 149. Roethlisberger 1979, vol. 1, pp. 351-52, no. 149, vol. 2, fig. 246. Rowan 1991, pp. 173-83.

JACQUES~LOUIS DAVID

The Funeral of Patroclus, 1779

Provenance: Sold by the artist to Abraham Fontanel, Paris, 12 March, 1782 for 2,400 livres (del Caso, 1972, p. 686); Acton Collection, Naples; Serra, Duca del Cardinale, Naples (prior to 1840); Heim Gallery, London, where purchased, 1973 for £250,000.

Exhibitions: 1778 Rome. 1781 Paris, no. 314. 1974-75 Paris etc., no. 27. 1981-82 Rome, no. 22. 1985 London, no. 16. 1989-90 Paris, no. 31.

NGI Catalogues: Potterton 1981, p. 33.

Selected References: Diderot 1781, ed. Seznec and Adhémar 1967, vol. 4, pp. 351, 378. David 1867, pp. 32, 40. David 1880, pp. 12, 22-23, 632. Rosenberg 1970, p. 36, under no. 20. Rosenberg 1973, pp. 78-79. Rosenblum 1973, pp. 567-78. Wildenstein 1973, nos. 43, 45, 88, 98, 1368, 1810, 1938. Rosenblum 1974-75, exh. cat., no. 27. Sérullaz 1974-75, under no. 13. Howard 1975, pp. 59-61, 89. Schnapper 1989-90, exh. cat., pp. 88, 89, 563, no. 31 (with complete bibliography), under nos. 30, 32, 33. Rosenblum 1991, pp. 166-71.

WILLEM DROST

Bust of a Man Wearing a Large-Brimmed Hat, c.1654

Provenance: Purchased by Joseph Strutt of Derby between 1820 and 1821; thence by descent to Howard Galton of Hadzor by 1854; by descent to Hubert Galton; his sale (Hadzor Sale) Christie's, 22 June 1889, lot 26, where purchased for 96 guineas.

Exhibitions: 1857 Manchester, no. 676. 1882 Worcester, no. 72. 1883 London, no. 64. 1983 Amsterdam and Groningen, no. 20. 1987 Santa Ana, etc., no. 11.

NGI Catalogues: Potterton 1981, p. 42 (as van den Eeckhout). Potterton 1986, pp. 35-36.

Selected References: Strutt 1827. Waagen 1854, vol. 3 p. 221. Armstrong 1890, p. 286. Duncan 1906-07, p. 16. Potterton 1982, p. 104 and n. 6-10, p. 107. Sumowski 1983-, vol. 1, no. 328, p. 615. 1983 Amsterdam/Groningen, no. 20, p. 130.

WILLEM CORNELISZ. DUYSTER

Interior with Soldiers, 1632

Provenance: 1895 purchased from Dermot Bourke, 7th Earl of Mayo.

NGI Catalogues: Armstrong 1898, p. 43. Potterton 1981, p. 39. Potterton 1986, pp. 41-42.

Selected References: Duncan 1906-07, p. 17.

CONRAD FABER

Katherina Knoblauch, 1532

Provenance: Henry Farrer sale, Christie's, London, 15-16 June 1866, lot 289, where purchased for 23 guineas.

Exhibitions: 1885 London, no. 174. 1906 London, no. 26. 1985 London, no. 20.

NGI Catalogues: Potterton 1981, p. 49. Oldfield 1987, pp. 20-24.

Selected References: Von Lersner 1706, vol. I, pp. 103, 115, 120. Braune 1909, p. 582. Friedländer 1913, p. 147 (no. 9). Collins Baker 1920, p. 194. Hugelshofer 1939a, p. 19. Brücker 1965, pp. 12, 42-44, 86, 134, 171-72, no. 17. Laver 1969, p. 80, pl. 78. Dülberg 1990, p. 193, no. 55.

THOMAS GAINSBOROUGH

A View in Suffolk, c.1746

Provenance: By c.1850 J.H. Reynolds; by descent to F.W. Reynolds; 10 April 1883, purchased at Christie's, London, Reynolds sale, lot 109.

Exhibitions: 1934 Manchester, no. 43. 1934 London, no. 310. 1936 Amsterdam, no. 39. 1938 Paris, no. 45. 1962 Nottingham, no. 4. 1967 Kenwood, no. 8. 1977 Bordeaux, no. 7. 1980-81 London, no. 77. 1981 Paris, no. 14.

NGI Catalogues: Doyle 1890, p. 53. Armstrong 1898, p. 51. Potterton 1981, p. 59.

Selected References: Armstrong 1894, p. 76. Armstrong 1898a, pp. 38, 67, 69, 306, ill. facing p. 12. Boulton 1905, pp. 47, 48, 62. Menpes and Grieg 1909, p. 48. Royal Academy 1935, no. 178, pl. 63. Woodall 1935, p. 45. Woodall 1939, p. 15. Millar 1949, p. 6, pl. 10. Woodall 1949, pp. 25-26, ill. Waterhouse 1958, p. 110, no. 870. Woodall 1962, p. 562. Hayes 1970, vol. 2, p. 136. Hayes 1975, p. 201, no. 4, pl. 5. Piper 1975, pp. 186-87. Lindsay 1981, pp. 22-23. Hayes 1982, vol. 1, pp. 46, 47, 48, 57, 164, 167, pl. 1, fig. 55; vol. 2, pp. 338-39, no. 13, 341.

ORAZIO GENTILESCHI

David and Goliath, c.1605-06

Provenance: A small sweetshop in the Limehouse area of London, where purchased by Tomás Harris, London, from whom purchased in 1936 for £1,400.

Exhibitions: 1951 Milan, no. 108. 1985 London, no. 4. 1992 Dublin, no. 4.

NGI Catalogues: Potterton 1981, p. 61. Wynne 1986, pp. 37-39.

Selected References: Longhi 1943, p. 22. Emiliani 1958, p. 43. Schleier 1962, pp. 432-36. Wittkower 1973, p. 43. Bissell 1981, p. 146. Garstang 1987, p. 152. Brigstocke 1988, p. 40. Berti 1991, pp. 15 and 17, fig. 6.

BARON FRANÇOIS~PASCAL~SIMON GÉRARD

Julie Bonaparte as Queen of Spain with her Daughters, Zénaïde and Charlotte, 1808-09

Provenance: Joseph Bonaparte, King of Naples and Spain; Zénaïde, Princess of Canino; Cardinal Lucien Bonaparte; Marchesa Julie di Roccagiovine and her descendants; Heim Gallery, London, where purchased 1972 for £40,000.

Exhibitions: 1972 London, no. 20. 1985 London, no. 17.

NGI Catalogues: Potterton 1981, p. 61.

Selected References: Gérard 1852-57, vol. 1, pl. 22. Lenormant 1847, p. 182. Gérard 1886, vol. II, p. 404. Bertin 1893, pp. 24, 91,

418. Pératé 1909-10, p. 7. Valynseele 1954, pp. 41-43. Ansaldi 1955, p. 38. de l'Ain 1970, p. 351, no. 1. Constans 1980, p. 59. Latreille 1989, p. 228.

FRANCISCO DE GOYA Y LUCIENTES

'El Conde del Tajo', c.1800

Provenance: Marquis de la Vega Inclán, Madrid; Sulley & Co., from whom purchased in 1908 for £975.

Exhibitions: 1911 London, no. 53. 1954-55 London, no. 359. 1963-64 London, no. 75. 1985 London, no. 12.

NGI Catalogues: Armstrong 1914, p. 55. Potterton 1981, p. 63. Mulcahy 1988, pp. 17-18.

Selected References: Zapater y Gómez 1924, pl. 185 (as 'Desconocido'). Mayer 1924, no. 429, pl. 176. Gaya Nuño 1958, no. 935. Gudiol 1971, vol. 1, p. 119, no. 454, p. 296. De Angelis 1974, no. 756. Camón Aznar 1980, vol. 3, p. 31. Glendinning 1980, p. 357.

JAN DAVIDSZ. DE HEEM

A Vanitas *Fruit-piece*, 1653

Provenance: By 1754, Lucas de Schamp, Ghent and thence by descent; 14 September 1840, Schamp D'Aveschoot sale, Rogemorter, Ghent, lot 133; 7-9 November 1863, George Blamire sale, Christie's, London, lot 49, where purchased for 65 guineas.

Exhibitions: 1987 Santa Ana etc., no. 17. 1991 Utrecht and Braunschweig, no. 27.

NGI Catalogues: Potterton 1981, p. 71. Potterton 1986, pp. 59-60.
Selected References: Descamps 1753-64, vol. 2 (1754), p. 40. Armstrong 1890, p. 283. Greindl 1956, pp. 122, 172. Brochhagen and Knüttel 1967, p. 32. de Mirimonde 1971, pp. 268, 271, fig. 15. Hairs 1985, vol. 2, p. 29. Grimm 1988, pp. 225, 227, fig. 166. Segal 1988, pp. 113, 116, 215, fig. 6.10.

MEINDERT HOBBEMA

A Wooded Landscape - The Path on the Dyke, 1663

Provenance: Edward John Littleton (later Lord Hatherton) by 1828 when lent to the British Institution. The painting is said by Smith to have been painted for an ancestor of Littleton. Purchased from Lord Hatherton by Lord Dudley sometime between 1857 and 1864; Earl of Dudley sale, London, 25 June 1892, lot 7, bt. Agnew, from whom purchased, 6 March 1895 by Alfred Beit; by descent in 1906 to his brother Otto, later Sir Otto Beit, Bt.; by descent in 1930 to his son, Sir Alfred Beit, Bt. Presented by Sir Alfred and Lady Beit, 1987 (Beit Collection).

Exhibitions: 1828 British Institution, no. 122. 1857 Manchester, no. 722 (lent by Lord Hatherton). 1864 British Institution, no. 30 (lent by Lord Dudley). 1871 London, no. 377. 1900 London, no. 11. 1908 London, no. 69. 1929 London, no. 155. 1949-50 Capetown, no. 14. 1957 Manchester. 1970-71 The Hague and London, no. 68. 1988 Dublin, no. 4.

NGI Catalogues: Beit 1988, pp. 20-21.

Selected References: Smith 1829-42, Part 6, no. 1, pp. 114-15. Waagen 1854, vol. 2, p. 251. Hofstede de Groot 1908-27, vol. 4, no. 136, p. 400. Bode 1913, p. 21, no. 28, p. 76. Rosenberg 1927. Broulhiet 1938, no. 304, p. 418, repr. p. 254 and fig. 570, p. 369. Watson 1960, p. 158. Rosenberg, Slive and ter Kuile 1966, p. 157. Sutton 1987, pp. 348-49.

WILLIAM HOGARTH

The Mackinen Children, 1747

Provenance: Presumed commissioned by William Mackinen (c.1697-1767) for his home on the Island of Antigua; 1798 returned to England and by family descent at Binfield, Berkshire, to widow of Major-General Daniel Henry Mackinnon; c.1900 purchased by Sir Hugh Lane, by whom bequeathed, 1915, and received in the Gallery (Lane Bequest), 1918.

Exhibitions: 1918 Dublin, no. 22. 1965 Kenwood, no. 6. 1975 Tokyo, no. 13. 1979-80 Stockholm, no. 123. 1989 Venice, no. 145.

NGI Catalogues: Potterton 1981, p. 75.

Selected References: Oliver 1896, vol. 1, p. 259. Mandel 1967, p. 116, no. 2:D, ill. (as probably not Hogarth). Bisutti and Contini 1976, p. 56, pl. 4. Paulson 1971, vol. 1, front., pp. 225, 458, 459, 556n, fig. 179; vol. 2, p. 242. Lindsay 1977, p. 118, ill. Johnson 1986, p. 52. Webster 1979, p. 118. Webster 1989, p. 151. Einberg 1989, p. 799.

WILLIAM HOGARTH

The Western Family, c.1738

Provenance: c.1738 presumed commissioned by Thomas Western of Rivenhall, Essex, and passed by descent; 13 June 1913, Sir Thomas C. Callis Western, Bt., sale, Christie's, London, lot 106, bt. Agnew's; c.1913 acquired by Sir Hugh Lane, by whom bequeathed, 1915, and received in the Gallery (Lane Bequest), 1918.

Exhibitions: 1814 London, no. 92. 1865 London, no. 150. 1867a London, no. 351. 1918 Dublin, no. 28. 1934 Manchester, no. 10. 1934 London, no. 224. 1951 London, no. 42. 1954-55 London, no. 30. 1958 Dagenham. 1977 Bordeaux, no. 22.

NGI Catalogues: Potterton 1981, p. 75.

Selected References: Nichols et al 1781, p. 13, 1782, p. 12. Nichols and Steevens 1808-17, vol. 1, pp. 23, 399, vol. 3, pp. 179-80. Nichols 1833, p. 371. Dobson 1907, p. 223. Royal Academy 1935, pp. 19-20, no. 58, pl. 24. Sitwell 1936, p. 18, fig. 14. Beckett 1949, pp. 46-7, pl. 94. Mandel 1967, p. 103, no. 98. Paulson 1971, vol. 1, p. 225. Webster 1979, p. 89. Boydell 1985, p. 39.

WOLF HUBER

Anton Hundertpfundt, 1526

Provenance: Marquis de Blasil sale, Christie's, London, 17 May 1872, lot 127, where purchased for £40.

Exhibitions: 1885 London, no. 175. 1906 London, no. 49. 1965 Linz, no. 269.

NGI Catalogues: Potterton 1981, p. 77. Oldfield 1987, pp. 32-35.

Selected References: Conway 1885, p. 50. Voss 1907, p. 45. Habich 1908-09, p. 57. Stutzel 1911, pp. 27-31. Baldass 1922, p. 303. Voss 1925, vol. 18, pp. 21-22. Weinberger 1930, pp. 159-63, 233. Hugelshofer 1939a, p. 19. Hugelshofer 1939b, p. 233.

Heinzle 1953, no. 110. von der Osten and Vey 1969, p. 212. Rose 1977, pp. 9 (no. 17), 16, 250 (no. 328), 251. Winzinger 1979, vol. 1, pp. 182 (no. 298), 221. Dülberg 1990, p. 221 (no. 250).

MATHIEU LE NAIN (ATTRIBUTED TO)

Adoration of the Shepherds, 1644

Provenance: Dr. Mary collection; Heim Gallery, Paris from whom purchased, 1961 for £7,500.

Exhibitions: 1934 Paris, no. 48. 1960a Paris, no. 525.

NGI Catalogues: MacGreevy 1964, p. 77 (as Louis Le Nain). Potterton 1981, p. 96 (as Louis Le Nain).

Selected References: Jamot 1923, pp. 165, 166. Jamot 1929, pp. 115, 116. Fierens 1933, pp. 52 and 62, no. 7. Isarlo 1938, p. 36, no. 13. Thuillier 1961, p. 327 and 328. Thuillier 1978, pp. 50, 93, 117-118, 277. Blunt 1978, p. 873. Cuzin 1978, p. 876. Rosenberg 1979b, pp. 96, 98. Cuzin 1979, pp. 62, 63, 64, pl. 124. Wine 1992, p. 104.

FILIPPINO LIPPI (ATTRIBUTED TO)

Portrait of a Musician, 1480s

Provenance: Aldrovandi (Bologna); Ludovisi Boncompagni (Bologna/Rome); Princely collection, Rome; Lawrie and Co., London, 1897, from whom purchased for £1,500.

Exhibitions: 1902 London, no. 22. 1930 London, no. 240. 1949 Florence, no. 5.

NGI Catalogues: MacGreevy 1956, p. 72 (as Tura). Potterton 1981, p. 98 (as Filippino Lippi).

Selected References: Friedländer 1902, p. 143. Cook 1902, p. 118. *L'Arte* IX 1906, p. 480. Duncan 1906-07, p. 8. Venturi 1908, p. 432. *L'Arte,* 1910, p. 302. Gräff 1912, p. 219. Venturi vol. VII, pt. III (1914), pp. 542, 545 (fig. 410). Cook 1915a, pp. 102 (fig. d), 103. Venturi 1927, p. 163. Rossi 1930, p. 941. Venturi 1931. Marle 1931, vol. XII, pp. 296-97. Fiocco 1932, p. 342. Longhi 1934, p. 163. Ortolani 1941, p. 79. MacGreevy 1945, pp. 8-9. Hill 1951, pp. 261-92. Salmi 1957, p. 56. Berti and Baldini 1958, p. 79. Gamba 1958, pp. 63, 64, 89, 104. Ragghianti 1960, p. 17. Busignani 1962, p. 15. Salmi 1963, p. 61. Brown 1966, p. 396. Molajoli 1974, p. 90. Zeri 1974, pp. 92, 94, 95 (fig. 8). 1975 London, no. 2. Fahy 1976, p. 177. Ferretti 1978, p. 1245. Lightbown 1978, vol. 2, p. 34. Winternitz 1979, p. 90. Natale 1980, p. 51. Wackernagel 1981, p. 171. Arrighi 1983, p. 183. Calbi and Kelescian, 1984, p. 106. del Serra 1985, pp. 4-16. Boydell 1985, pp. 26-29. Campbell 1990, p. 98.

ANDREA MANTEGNA

Judith with the Head of Holofernes, c.1495-1500

Provenance: Purchased in Italy by the Hon. Lewis Wingfield; John Malcolm of Poltalloch; Lord Malcolm of Poltalloch, from whom purchased, per P. & D. Colnaghi, 1896 for £2,000.

Exhibitions: 1902 London, no. 46. 1930 London, no. 146. 1961 Mantua, no. 52. 1965 Jerusalem, no. 67. 1985 London, no. 1. 1992 London, no. 129.

NGI Catalogues: MacGreevy 1956, p. 44. Potterton 1981, p. 102.

Selected References: Kristeller 1901, p. 373, p. 368, fig. 129. Friedländer 1902, p. 143. *L'Arte,* 1906, p. 480. Duncan 1906-07, p. 7. Berenson 1910, pp. 48, 254. Venturi 1901-40, vol. 7, pt. 3, pp. 244, 247-48. Berenson 1931, p. 327. Bodkin 1956, p. 44. Paccagnini 1961, p. 71, no. 52, fig. 70. Bellonci and Garavaglia 1967, p. 114, no. 75. Oberhuber et al 1973, p. 338, no. 4. Zeri 1974, pp. 86, 98, 100 (fig. 21). Smith 1981, p. 10. 1983 Munich, p. 308. Christiansen 1992, for latest bibliography.

ANTON RAPHAEL MENGS

Thomas Conolly, 1758

Provenance: Commissioned by the sitter in Rome c. 1758; either this painting or the signed replica was seen by Horace Walpole in the house of the sitter's mother, Lady Anne Conolly, Grosvenor Square, London; hung in Long Gallery at Castletown, County Kildare, probably from the 1770s and passed by descent to the 6th Lord Carew, Castletown, from whom purchased by the Hon. Desmond Guinness, Leixlip Castle, County Kildare, circa 1966, from whom purchased 1983, for £15,000.

Exhibitions: 1984 Dublin, no. 15.

NGI Catalogues: Wynne 1986, pp. 74-75.

Selected References: Walpole 1937, vol. 5, p. 52. Boylan 1968, pp. 21-23. Guinness and Ryan 1971, p. 202. Röttgen 1977, p. 146, fig. 28. Russell 1978, pp. 10-11 and 16. Keller 1979, pp. 12 and 14.

GIOVAN BATTISTA MORONI

Portrait of a Gentleman and his Two Children, c.1565

Provenance: purchased London, 1866 (no details recorded) for £450.

Exhibitions: 1884 London, no. 159. 1978 London, no. 9. 1983-84 London, no. 63.

NGI Catalogues: Potterton 1981, p. 113.

Selected References: Duret 1882, p. 181. Richter 1884, p. 51. Armstrong 1890, pp. 232, 235. Duncan 1906-7, pp. 8, 11. Cook 1915b, pp. 235-36 (pl. 1a). Mather 1923, p. 423. Merten 1928, p. 37 (no. 68). Venturi 1929, vol. IX, pt. 4a, pp. 267, 269 (fig. 230), 276. Berenson 1931, p. 381. Lerndorff 1933, pp. 37, 41, 72 (no. 57), 73. Gamba 1934, p. 868. Cugini 1939 (repr. 1978), p. 318. Lerndorff 1939 (repr. 1978), pp. 89, 138, 139, 164. Mazza 1939, p. 30. Galetti and Camesasca 1951, vol. II, p. 1748. Cugini 1953, p. 3. Cappi Bentivegna 1962, p. 342, pl. 480. Kühnel-Kunze 1962, p. 93. Zeri 1974, p. 101. Gould 1978, p. 320. Spinelli 1978, p. 3. Brigstocke 1979, p. 96. Gregori and Rossi 1979, pp. 180, 181, 255-56 (no. 99) with full bibliography.

JAN MYTENS

A Lady Playing a Lute, 1648

Provenance: Acquired between 1827 and 1835 by Joseph Strutt of Derby; thence by descent to Howard Galton of Hadzor by 1854; thence by descent to Hubert Galton; his sale (Hadzor sale), Christie's, 22 June 1889, lot 51, where purchased for 40 guineas.

Exhibitions: 1857 Manchester, no. 618. 1882 Worcester, no. 358. 1969 Bordeaux, no. 51. 1985 London, no. 33. 1987 Santa Ana, California, etc., no. 26.

NGI Catalogues: Potterton 1981, p. 115. Potterton 1986, pp. 102-03.

Selected References: Waagen 1854, vol. 3, p. 222. Boydell 1985, pp. 29-32.

JEAN~BAPTISTE PERRONNEAU

Portrait of a Man, 1766

Provenance: Thos. Agnew & Sons, from whom purchased, 1929 for £2,000.

Exhibitions: 1932 London, no. 236. 1932 Manchester, no. 95. 1968 London, no. 552. 1985 London, no. 15.

NGI Catalogues: Potterton 1981, p. 126.

Selected References: Milford 1932, p. 58, no. 221. Kalnein and Levey 1972, p. 131.

NICOLAS POUSSIN

The Holy Family with Saint Anne, Saint Elizabeth and the Young Saint John, 1649

Provenance: Painted for Jean Pointel in 1649 (Félibien 1685), figured in the latter's posthumous inventory, 20-22 December 1660, estimated at 400 livres (Thuiller and Mignot 1978); collection of Cerisier (or Serisier), another dealer friend of Poussin, at whose home G.L. Bernini saw the painting on 10 August 1665 (Chantelou); collection of the Earls of Milltown, Russborough House (Neale 1826); Milltown Gift, 1902.

Exhibitions: 1847 Dublin. 1916 Dublin, no. 55. 1962 Bologna, no. 78. 1985 Dublin, no. 35.

NGI Catalogues: Potterton 1981, p. 129.

Selected References: Félibien 1685, p. 299 (ed. 1725, IV, p. 59). Neale 1826, n.p. Chantelou 1885, p. 990 (cf. ed. 1981, p. 103 and Thuillier 1960, p. 127). Grautoff 1914, vol. I, pp. 271-73, vol. II, pp. 208-209. Friedlaender and Blunt 1939, pp. 22, no. D2(a) and 27 under no. 52. Blunt 1960a, under no. 86. Blunt 1960b, p. 400. Thuillier 1960, vol. II, p. 127 (text of Chantelou) and n.15. Mahon 1961, p. 129. Mahon 1962, pp. 116-118 and 117 fig. 41. Friedlaender 1965, pp. 60 fig. 57, 63. Blunt 1966, pp. 43-44, no. 59. Blunt 1967, vol. II, p. 208. Hibbard 1974, pp. 88, 89 fig. 56. Thuillier 1974, p. 105 under no. 164. Blunt 1974, p. 761. Thuillier and Mignot 1978, pp. 48-49. Wild 1980, vol. II, p. 140, no. 50. Wright 1985, no. 143. Laveissière 1985, no. 35 (with complete bibliography).

NICOLAS POUSSIN

The Lamentation over the Dead Christ, 1655-60

Provenance: (?) Listed in the inventory of the painter Samuel Bossière (1620-1703), drawn up by the artist (De Laroque 1872, p. 28) as *Christ que l'on va mettre au sépulcre*; (?) The Adriaan Bout sale, The Hague, 11th August 1733, lot 6 (38 x 54 ins.); (?) acquired by Sir William Hamilton in Rome, c. 1780 (Grautoff 1914, vol. 2, no. 113); Hamilton Palace sale, Christie's, London, 17th July and ff., 1882, lot 1120, where purchased for £503.

Exhibitions: 1932 London, no. 120. 1937 Paris, no. 115. 1960b Paris, no. 96. 1962 Bologna, no. 84. 1977-78 Rome and Düsseldorf, no. 42. 1985 London, no. 13.

NGI Catalogues: Potterton 1981, p. 129.

Selected References: Smith 1837, part 8, p. 60, no. 121. Waagen 1854-57, vol. 3, p. 300. Andresen 1863, no. A205. de Laroque 1872, p. 28. Friedlaender 1914, pp. 98, 256. Grautoff 1914, vol. 1, p. 228, vol. 2, no. 113. Magne 1914, p. 209, no.195. Bodkin 1932, p. 180. Wildenstein 1955, no. 69. Mahon 1960, p. 304, n. 107. Mahon 1962, pp. 118-19. Blunt 1966, vol. 1, p. 57, no. 83. Blunt 1967, vol. I, pp. 227, 301, 304, 306, 309. Thuillier 1974, p. 110, no. 206. Thuillier and Mignot 1978, p. 55. Rosenberg 1977-78, no. 42. Wild 1980, pp. 160, 178, no. 190. Cuzin et al 1983-84, p. 164. Wright 1985, no. 191.

MATTIA PRETI

The Beheading of Saint John the Baptist, c.1640

Provenance: Purchased in Rome in 1864 (no details recorded) for £100.

Exhibitions: 1992 Dublin, no. 12.

NGI Catalogues: Potterton 1981, p. 130. Wynne 1986, pp. 98-99.

Selected References: Whistler 1987, p. 67.

SIR JOSHUA REYNOLDS

The Earl of Bellamont, 1773-74

Provenance: In 1773 commissioned by the sitter; 1800 bequeathed to his illegitimate son, Sir Charles Coote, Bt. (1765-1857); 1857 bequeathed to his son, Sir Charles Coote; 3 July 1875 Christie's, London, lot 51, where purchased for £550.

Exhibitions: 1774 London, no. 219. 1985 Paris, no. 39. 1985-86 London, no. 89.

NGI Catalogues: Doyle 1890, p. 106. Armstrong 1898, p. 121. Armstrong 1904, p. 278. Potterton 1981, p. 136.

Selected References: *Public Advertiser* 1774. Lewis 1837, vol. 1, p. 33. Leslie and Taylor 1865, vol. 2, pp. 46-7. Graves and Cronin 1899-1901, vol. 1, p. 79. Whitley 1928, vol. 2, p. 295. Waterhouse 1941, p. 64, pl. 156. Cormack 1970, p. 147. Burke 1976, p. 206. Penny and Mannings 1986, pp. 761-62. Luna 1989, pp. 368-69, ill.

JACOB VAN RUISDAEL

The Castle of Bentheim, 1653

Provenance: According to Smith, said traditionally to have been painted expressly for the Count of Bentheim, in whose family it is said to have remained until the entrance of the French into Germany about which time it was taken to Paris and thence to England, becoming the property of William Smith, M.P. (by 1815); consigned by Smith to Buchanan and 'afterwards passed into the possession of a gentleman at Bristol', Thomas Kebble of Green Trees, near Tonbridge, Kent by 1835; A Nobleman (Thomas Kebble) sale, London, 2 June 1856, lot 54, bt. Woodin for John Walter, Bearwood; presumed to have been purchased from there by Alfred Beit sometime between 1895 and his death in 1906 and probably at the same time as Steen's *Marriage Feast at Cana* which was before 1900. By descent in 1906 to his brother Otto, later Sir Otto Beit, Bt.; by descent in 1930 to his son, Sir Alfred Beit, Bt. Presented by Sir Alfred and Lady Beit, 1987 (Beit Collection).

Exhibitions: 1815 London, no. 94 (lent by W. Smith). 1857 Manchester, no. 708 (lent by J. Walter). 1861 London, no. 50. 1868 Leeds, no. 792. 1907 London, no. 8 (lent by O. Beit). 1929 London, no 95. 1935 Brussels, no. 764. 1949-50 Capetown, no. 25. 1967 London. 1981-82 The Hague and Harvard University, no. 14. 1988 Dublin, no. 14.

NGI Catalogues: Beit 1988, pp. 44-46.

Selected References: Buchanan 1824, vol. 2, p. 360. Smith 1835, Part 6, no. 258, pp. 81-82. Waagen 1854-57, p. 296. Burger 1865, p. 295. Michel 1910, pp. 148 ff, and repr. pl. 9. Hofstede de Groot 1908-27, vol. 4, no. 25, p. 15. Bode 1913, pp. 18-19, no. 50, p. 81. Rosenberg 1928, no. 18. Watson 1960, p. 158. Gotker 1964, pp. 96-100. Rosenberg, Slive, ter Kuile 1966, p. 156. Korn 1978, pp. 111-14. Maschmayer 1978, pp. 61-71. Hagels 1968, p. 46. Wiegand 1971, pp. 93-98. Slive 1981-82, no. 14, pp. 54-55. Bruyn 1987, pp. 98-99. Schneider 1990, pp. 80-81. Walford 1991, p. 86. Sutton 1992, pp. 165-69.

GOTFRIED SCHALCKEN

Preciosa Recognised, late 1660s

Provenance: In the collection of Philippe, Duc d'Orléans (the Regent) at the Palais-Royal, Paris which was formed in the quarter of a century before the Duke's death in 1723. It remained at the Palais-Royal until the Flemish and Dutch paintings of the collection were sold by the great-grandson of the Duc d'Orléans ('Philippe-Égalité') in 1791 or 1792 to Thomas Moore Slade, acting on behalf of Lord Kinnaird, Mr. Morland and Mr. Hammersley. These paintings were brought to England in 1792 and no. 476 was exhibited with them for sale by private contract in London, April-June 1793. It was sold for £100 at that time. 'A Gentleman of Surrey' (Stephenson) sale, Christie's. 26 May 1818, lot 156, bt. in; Albert Levy sale, Christie's, 6 April 1876, lot 367, bt. Pearson, P & D Colnaghi, from whom purchased, 1898, for £150.

Exhibitions: 1793 London, no. 38.

NGI Catalogues: Armstrong 1908, pp. 145-46. Potterton 1981, p. 147. Potterton 1986, pp. 141-42.

Selected References: de Saint Gelais 1727, pp. 443-44. Descamps 1760, p. 143. Smith 1833, no. 95, p. 286. Hofstede de Groot 1913, no. 88, p. 334. Gaskell 1982, p. 270 and n. 63. Beherman 1988, no. 49, p. 142.

JAN STEEN

The Village School, c.1663-65

Provenance: Izaak Hoogenbergh sale, Hayman, Amsterdam, 10 April 1743, lot 42, bt. W. Lormier; W. Lormier sale, The Hague, 4 July 1763, lot 246; probably Greffier Fagel, The Hague; thence by descent to the Countess of Holderness; probably Countess of Holderness, decd. sale, Christie's, 6 March 1802, lot 110, bt. Dermer; 'Property of a Gentleman' sale, Christie's, 8 February 1806, lot 105; G.J. Cholmondeley by 1818; G.J. Cholmondeley sale, Squibb, London, 23 April 1831, lot 15; Colnaghi, from whom purchased, 1879, for £420.

Exhibitions: probably 1818 London, no. 108. 1883 London, no. 249. 1929 London no. 241. 1952-53 London, no. 573. 1956-57 Rome, no. 286. 1958-59 The Hague, no. 311. 1966-67 San Francisco, no. 90. 1984, Philadelphia etc., no. 107.

NGI Catalogues: Potterton 1981, p. 155. Potterton 1986, pp. 145-48.

Selected References: Hoet 1752, vol. 2, p. 438. Buchanan 1824, vol. 1, no. 63, p. 316. Smith 1829-42, Part 4, nos. 21 and 22, pp. 7-8. van Westrheene 1856, no. 240, p. 148. Armstrong 1890, p. 283. Duncan 1906-07, p. 18. Hofstede de Groot 1908-27, vol. 1, nos. 285, p. 81 and 300, p. 84. Bredius 1927, p. 23. Rosenberg, Slive, ter Kuile 1966, p. 135. de Vries 1977, p. 57 and no. 116, p. 164. Braun 1980, no. 198, p. 114. Durantini 1983, p. 120 and pp. 158-60.

JAN STEEN

The Marriage Feast at Cana, late 1660s

Provenance: A. van Hoek sale, Amsterdam, 7 April 1806; sale at Bicker and Wijkersloot, Amsterdam, 19 July 1809, lot 51, bt. Spaan; Delahante sale, Phillips, London, 2 June 1814, lot 37, bt. Woodburn (£120.15); Constantine sale, Paris, 1829, bt. Nieuwenhuys; Nieuwenhuys sale, Christie's, London, 11 May 1833, lot 117, bt. Norton (£194.5); Lord Northwick sale, Christie's, London, 24 May 1838, lot 100, bt. Clowes (£294); Casimer Perier sale, Christie's, London, 5 May 1848, lot 14, bt. Woodin; J. Walter, Bearwood, from whom purchased by Alfred Beit between 1895 and 1900 (when lent to Burlington Fine Arts Club). (Note: both Kirschenbaum and Braun state incorrectly that the picture was in the Lansdowne collection at Bowood subsequent to being in the Walter collection); by descent in 1906 to his brother Otto, later Sir Otto Beit, Bt,; by descent in 1930 to his son, Sir Alfred Beit, Bt. Presented by Sir Alfred and Lady Beit, 1987 (Beit Collection).

Exhibitions: 1837 London, no. 174. 1857 Manchester, no. 946. 1862 London, no. 69. 1882 London, no. 55 (lent by J. Walter). 1900 London, no. 44 (lent by A. Beit). 1909 London, no. 5. 1926 Leiden, no. 23. 1929 London, no. 206. 1945 Nottingham, no. 56. 1949-50 Capetown, no. 28. 1952 Capetown, no. 28. 1957 Dublin, no. 157. 1958-59 The Hague, no. 51. 1988 Dublin, no. 15.

NGI Catalogues: Beit 1988, pp. 47-9.

Selected References: Smith 1835, Part 4, no. 100, pp. 31-2 and idem. Suppl. 52. Van Westrheene 1856, no. 85. Waagen 1854-57, p. 296. Hofstede de Groot 1908-27, vol. 1, nos. 48 and 49, pp. 20-21. Holmes 1909, p. 243. Martin 1909, pp. 156-58. Bode 1913, pp. 14-15 and no. 57, p. 83. Van Gelder 1926, p. 210. Bredius 1927, p. 32. Schmidt-Degener and van Gelder 1927, pp. 11-12 and p. 34. Brière-Misme 1928, p. 289. Martin 1927-28, p. 332. Stechow 1928-29, p. 175. Fischel 1935, p. 65. Heppner 1939-40, pp. 43-44. Gudlaugsson 1945, p. 6. Bax 1951, pp. 261 ff. Bax 1952, pp. 113-15. de Groot 1952, pp. 81, 153 and 181-82. Martin 1954, p. 40. Watson 1960, p. 158. Stechow 1972, pp. 73-83. Kirschenbaum 1977, no. 48/49, pp. 21, 98, 131-33. Braun 1980, no. 329.

BERNARDO STROZZI

Spring and Summer, c.1640

Provenance: Alessandro Aducci, Rome, from whom purchased 1836 by Richard, 6th Viscount Powerscourt, Powerscourt, County Wicklow; Harris and Sinclair, Dublin, by 1924, when purchased for £350.

Exhibitions: 1950-51 London, no 402. 1959 Venice, no. 81. 1979 London, no. 26. 1986 Genoa, no. 4.

NGI Catalogues: Potterton 1981, p. 157. Wynne 1986, pp. 117-18.

Selected References: Powerscourt 1903, p. 53. Mortari 1966, fig. 475. Whistler 1987, p. 67.

GIOVANNI BATTISTA TIEPOLO

Allegory of the Immaculate Conception, 1769

Provenance: Probably brought back from Madrid to Venice by Giovanni Domenico Tiepolo after his father's death in 1770; appeared on Venetian market after his own death in 1804; purchased by Duke of Portland in Venice c.1870-90; G.A.F. Cavendish Bentick sale, Christie's 13 July 1891, and following days, lot 771, where purchased for 50 guineas.

Exhibitions: 1960 Coventry, no. 43; 1985 London, no. 10.

NGI Catalogues: Armstrong 1908, p. 163. Potterton 1981, p. 162. Wynne 1986, pp. 119-21.

Selected References: Morassi 1962, p. 11. Pallucchini 1968, no. 287. Whistler 1985, pp. 172-73. Levey 1986, p. 283.

TIZIANO VECELLIO, CALLED TITIAN

Ecce Homo, late 1550s

Provenance: Van Dyck (?); Sir William Knighton sale, Christie's, London, 21 May 1885 and ff., lot 520, where purchased for £70 18s.

Exhibitions: 1883 London, no. 182. 1955 Birmingham, no. 107. 1985 London, no. 2.

NGI Catalogues: MacGreevy 1956, p. 70. Potterton 1981, p. 164.

Selected References: Duncan 1906-07, p. 7. Gore 1955, pp. 194 (fig. 1), 218. Berenson 1957, vol. 1, p. 185. Ionescu 1960, pp. 38-45, ills.. Valcanover 1960, vol. 2, p. 69. Ionescu 1961, ills. p. 279, fig. 3. Cagli and Valcanover 1969, p. 128, no. 413. Pallucchini 1969, text p. 158, cat. p. 305 (no. 422). Wethey 1969, pp. 87-88 (no. 34). Wethey 1972, vol. II, pp. 753-7. Zeri 1974, pp. 100, 102 (fig. 24). Fisher 1977, pp. 85, 88, no. 85. Heinemann 1980, pp. 436, 440. Hope 1980, p. 122 (*Ecce Homo* for CV). Pérez Sánchez 1980, p. 354. Rearick 1980, p. 373. Pignatti 1981, vol. 2, p. 32, no. 381.

CORNELIS TROOST

Jeronimus Tonneman and his son Jeronimus: The Dilettanti, 1736

Provenance: Jeronimus Tonneman the Younger; by descent to his daughter Mrs. P.H. de la Court; thence by descent; coll. Douaire de la Court-Ram, Utrecht, 1894; J. van Citters sale, Christie's, 12 June 1899, lot 78, bt. Dowdeswell; coll. Ward, London; S. Richards, London, from whom purchased, 1909, for £120.

Exhibitions: 1894 Utrecht, no. 440. 1948 Rotterdam, no. 106. 1952 Amsterdam, no. 169. 1954-55 London, no. 113. 1971-72 Minneapolis etc. no. 89. 1985 London, no. 34.

NGI Catalogues: Potterton 1981, p. 165. Potterton 1986, pp. 155-56.

Selected References: Duncan 1906-07, p. 18. Henkell 1939, p. 426. Knoef 1947a, p. 20. Knoef 1947b, pp. 14-15. Staring 1956, p. 110. Rosenberg, Slive, ter Kuile 1966, p. 213. Praz 1971, p. 173. Niemeijer 1973, no. 136S, pp. 204-05. de Jongh 1972-73, p. 79. Boydell 1985, pp. 32-33. 1985 London, no. 34, p. 84.

DIEGO DE SILVA VELÁZQUEZ

Kitchen Maid with the Supper at Emmaus, c.1618-19

Provenance: Exported from Spain to England at some unknown date; according to a label on the reverse, in the collection of the Rev. Swiney, allegedly in the possession of Sir Hugh Lane, c.1909; in the collection of Sir Otto Beit, Belgrave Square, London, by 1913; by descent in 1930, to his son, Sir Alfred Beit, Bt. Presented by Sir Alfred and Lady Beit, 1987 (Beit Collection).

Exhibitions: 1913-14 London, no. 41 (where attributed to Velázquez for the first time). 1920-21 London, no 65. 1947 London, no. 29. 1955 Bordeaux, no. 61. 1956-57 Rome, no. 303. 1957 Dublin, no. 77. 1960-61 Madrid, no. 29. 1988 Dublin, no. 16. 1990 Madrid, no. 1.

NGI Catalogues: Mulcahy 1988, pp. 79-82. Beit 1988, pp. 50-53.

Selected References: Beruete y Moret 1913, pp. 127-28. Beruete y Moret 1914, p. 68. Mayer 1927, p. 562-63. Allende-Salazar 1925, no. 1. Mayer 1936, no. 106. Lafuente Ferrari 1943, no. 3, appendix A; 1944 ed., no. 5. Trapier 1948, p. 72. Soria 1949, p. 127. Justi 1953, p. 818. Gaya Nuño 1953, no. 5. Ortega y Gasset 1954, no. 10, p. 53. Pantorba 1955, no. 4, p. 65. Gerstenberg 1957, p. 24. Gaya Nuño 1958, no. 2814, pp. 317-18. López-Rey 1963, pp. 32-33, 127-28, no. 18. Camón Aznar 1964, pp. 252-55. López-Rey 1968, p. 34. Haraszti-Tackács 1973, pp. 34-35. López-Rey 1979, pp. 216-17, no. 17. Asturias and Bardi 1977, no. 5. Harris 1982, pp. 44-46. Haraszti-Tackács 1983, p. 89 and no. 214, p. 224. C. Brown 1984, p. 21. Brown 1986, pp. 21, 278, no. 10. Wind 1987, pp. 24-25, 31-33, 96-98. Ortiz et al 1989, pp. 27-29.

SIMON VOUET

The Four Seasons, c.1644-45

Provenance: Collection of W.P. Odlum at Huntington, Portarlington; acquired from Mr. Neville Orgel in London, 1970 for £24,000.

Exhibitions: 1985 Dublin, no. 41. 1990-91 Paris, no. 59.

NGI Catalogues: Potterton 1981, p. 175.

Selected References: Crelly 1962, p. 254, no. 233 (lost painting; catalogues the engraving as *Allegorie de la Fecondité* [?]). Donald 1970, pp. 14, 19 (engraving; *La Chronique des Arts* 1971, supplement to *Gazette des Beaux-Arts,* I, February, p. 133, no. 613). Crelly 1981, pp. 401-24, cf. p. 403, fig. 4. Boeckh 1982, pp. 99-101, fig. 71. Thuillier 1990-91, p. 328, no. 59.

JAN BAPTIST WEENIX

The Sleeping Shepherdess, c.1656-58

Provenance: Duke of Brunswick-Wolfenbuttel, Salzthalum until 1795; François-Xavier de Burtin, 1808; Etienne Le Roy, from whom acquired in 1855 by Vicomte du Bus de Gisignies; his sale, Brussels, 9-10 May 1882, lot 91; where purchased by Sir Henry Page Turner Barron, by whom bequeathed, 1901.

Exhibition: 1987 Santa Ana, etc., no. 34.

NGI Catalogues: Potterton 1981, p. 177. Potterton 1986, pp. 174-75.

Selected References: de Burtin 1808, vol. 2, p. 347. Fétis 1878, p. 196. Kreplin 1942, p. 246. Ginnings 1970, no. 67, p. 185. Blankert 1978, n. 2 of no. 102, p. 182 and n. 2 of no. 105, p. 184. Schloss 1983, p. 79. Salomon 1987, pp. 315-45.

FRANCIS WHEATLEY

The Marquess and Marchioness of Antrim, 1782

Provenance: Presumably commissioned by the 6th Earl of Antrim (later 1st Marquess); by descent to his younger daughter, Charlotte, *suo jure* Countess of Antrim (1779-1835); 1835 bequeathed to her daughter Lady Louisa Letitia Kerr; bequeathed to her great-nephew and godchild A.R. MacGregor; bequeathed to his son, Lt. Commander M.F. MacGregor, by whom sold at auction, 21 November 1980, Christie's, London, lot 60, where purchased for £110,000.

Exhibition: Dublin 1981, no. 12.

NGI Catalogues: Potterton 1981, p. 179.

Selected References: Webster 1984, pp. 42-45.

FRANCISCO DE ZURBARÁN

The Immaculate Conception, early 1660s

Provenance: Possibly from Valladolid; first recorded in England in 1872 when sold by Captain Larkyns; W. Graham sale, Christie's, 10 April 1886, lot. 408 (as Valdés Leal), where purchased for 42 guineas.

Exhibition: 1981a London, no. 40.

NGI Catalogues: Potterton 1981, p. 186. Mulcahy 1988, pp. 89-91.

Selected References: Mayer 1922, p. 42. Gaya Nuño 1958, no. 3146, p. 347. Guinard 1960, no. 17. Mulcahy 1984, p. 33.

BIBLIOGRAPHY

de l'Ain 1970
G. Girod de l'Ain, *Joseph Bonaparte, Le Roi Malgré Lui,* Paris 1970.

Allende-Salazar 1925
J. Allende-Salazar, ed., *Velázquez. Des Meisters Gemälde,* vol. 4 of Klassiker der Kunst, 4th ed., Berlin, Leipzig 1925.

Andresen 1863
A. Andresen, *Nicolas Poussin, Verzeichniss der nach seinen Gemälden gefertigten gleichzeitigen und Späteren Kupferstiche,* Leipzig 1863, reprinted *Gazette des Beaux-Arts,* July-Aug 1962, pp. 139-202.

de Angelis 1974
R. de Angelis, *L'Opera Pittorica Completa di Goya,* Milan 1974.

Ansaldi 1955
G. R. Ansaldi, 'Ritratti inediti di Wicar', *Bollettino dei Musei Communali di Roma,* nos. 3-4, 1955.

Armstrong 1890
W. Armstrong, 'The National Gallery of Ireland - I', *The Magazine of Art,* 1890.

Armstrong 1894
W. Armstrong, *Thomas Gainsborough,* London 1894.

Armstrong 1898
W. Armstrong, *Catalogue of Pictures and other works of art in the National Gallery and National Portrait Gallery, Ireland,* Dublin 1898.

Armstrong 1898a
W. Armstrong, *Gainsborough and his Place in English Art,* London 1898 and 1904.

Armstrong 1904
W. Armstrong, *Catalogue of Pictures and other works of art in the National Gallery and National Portrait Gallery, Ireland,* Dublin 1904.

Armstrong 1908
W. Armstrong, *Catalogue of Pictures and other works of art in the National Gallery and National Portrait Gallery, Ireland,* Dublin 1908.

Armstrong 1914
W. Armstrong, *Catalogue of Pictures and other works of art in the National Gallery and National Portrait Gallery, Ireland,* Dublin 1914.

Arrighi 1983
G. Arrighi, 'Pitture di Maestri Lucchesi della seconda metà del quattrocento e del principio del secolo successivo', *Castelli e Borghi della Toscana Tardo Medioevale,* Lucca 1983, pp.155-60.

L'Arte 1906
'Bibliografia', *L'Arte,* vol. 9, 1906, p. 480.

L'Arte 1910
'Corrieri, Esposizioni di antichi maestri a Londra', *L'Arte,* vol. 13, 1910, p. 302.

Asturias and Bardi 1977
M. A. Asturias and P. M. Bardi, *Velázquez,* Barcelona, Madrid 1977. (Spanish translation of Italian ed., Milan 1969).

Athenaeum 1902
'Old Masters at Burlington House, II', *The Athenaeum,* January 1902, pp. 89-90.

Baldass 1922
L. Baldass, 'A newly discovered portrait by Wolf Huber', *Burlington Magazine,* vol. 40, 1922, p. 303.

Baldinucci 1728
A. Baldinucci, *Notizie de'Professori del Disegno,* vol. 4, Florence, 1728. English translation in Roethlisberger 1979, pp. 53-62.

Bax 1951
D. Bax, *Skilders wat Vertal yn Uitleg van sewe Nederlandse en Vlaamse Sewentiende-eeuse Skilderye in Suid Afrikaanse Museums,* London, Capetown and New York 1951.

Bax 1952
D. Bax, *Hollandse en Vlaamse Schilderkunst in Zuid-Afrika,* Amsterdam 1952.

Beckett 1949
R. B. Beckett, *Hogarth,* London 1949.

Beherman 1988
T. S. Beherman, *Gotfried Schalcken,* Paris 1988.

Beit 1988
A. Le Harivel, R. Mulcahy and H. Potterton, *The Beit Collection,* Dublin 1988.

Bellonci and Garavaglia 1967
M. Bellonci and N. Garavaglia, *L'Opera Completa di Mantegna,* Milan 1967.

Berenson 1910
B. Berenson, *North Italian Painters,* New York and London 1910.

Berenson 1931
B. Berenson, *Italian Painters of the Renaissance,* Oxford 1931.

Berenson 1957
B. Berenson, *Italian Painters of the Renaissance: Venetian School,* London 1957.

Berti 1991
L. Berti, 'Artemisia da Roma tra i fiorentini', in *Artemisia,* Exhibition catalogue, Casa Buonarotti, Florence 1991, pp. 9ff.

Berti and Baldini 1958
L. Berti and U. Baldini, *Filippino Lippi,* Florence 1958.

Bertin 1893
G. Bertin, *Joseph Bonaparte en Amérique,* Paris 1893.

Beruete y Moret 1913
A. de Beruete y Moret, 'A hitherto unknown Velázquez', *Burlington Magazine,* vol. 24, December 1913, pp. 127-28.

Beruete y Moret 1914
A. de Beruete y Moret, 'Une exposition d'anciens maîtres Espagnols à Londres', *La Revue de l'Art,* vol. 35, 1914, pp. 61-75.

Bissell 1981
R. W. Bissell, *Orazio Gentileschi and the Poetic Tradition in Caraveggesque Painting,* London 1981.

Bisutti and Contini 1976
D. Bisutti and G. Contini, *I Geni dell'Arte: Hogarth,* Milan 1976.

Blankert 1978
A. Blankert, *Nederlandse 17e eeuwse Italianiserende landschapschilders,* Soest 1978.

Blankert 1982
A. Blankert, 'Hendrik Avercamp als schilder van winters', *Tableau,* 4, 1982, pp. 604-15.

Blunt 1954
A. Blunt, *The Drawings of G. B. Castiglione and Stefano della Bella in the Collection of Her Majesty the Queen at Windsor Castle,* London 1954.

Blunt 1960a
A. Blunt, *Nicolas Poussin,* Exhibition catalogue, 2 editions, Paris 1960.

Blunt 1960b
A. Blunt, 'Poussin Studies XI: Some addenda to the Poussin number', *Burlington Magazine,* vol. 102, September 1960, pp. 396-403, 489.

Blunt 1966
A. Blunt, *The Paintings of Nicolas Poussin, a critical catalogue,* 2 vols., Phaidon 1966.

Blunt 1967
A. Blunt, *Nicolas Poussin. The A. W. Mellon Lectures in the Fine Arts,* 1958, 2 vols., London and New York 1967.

Blunt 1974
A. Blunt, review of Thuillier 1974, *Burlington Magazine,* vol. 116, December 1974, pp. 760-63.

Blunt 1978
A. Blunt, review of Thuillier 1978, *Burlington Magazine,* vol. 120, December 1978, pp. 872-75.

Bocher 1876
E. Bocher, *Jean-Baptiste Siméon Chardin, Les Graveurs Françaises du XVIIIe siècle,* 3rd fasc., Paris 1876.

Bode 1913
W. Bode, *Catalogue of the Collection of Pictures and Bronzes in the possession of Mr Otto Beit,* London 1913.

Bodkin 1925
T. Bodkin, 'Chardin in the London and Dublin National Galleries', *Burlington Magazine,* vol. 47, July 1925, pp. 93-94.

Bodkin 1932
T. Bodkin, 'Nicolas Poussin in the National Gallery, Dublin', *Burlington Magazine,* vol. 60, April 1932, pp. 174-85.

Bodkin 1956
T. Bodkin, *Hugh Lane and His Pictures,* Dublin 1956.

Boeckh 1982
H. Boeckh, *Emailmalerei auf Genfer Taschenuhren vom 17. bis zum beginnenden 19. Jahrhundert,* Freiburg-im-Breisgau 1982.

Boulton 1905
W. B. Boulton, *Thomas Gainsborough, his Life, Works, Friends and Sitters,* London 1905.

Bouquier 1989-90
Bouquier, *Mes Matériaux,* cahier 1, p. 73, Paris, Arch. Ass. Pub. Ms. 141; quoted in Schnapper et al, 1989-90.

Boydell 1985
B. Boydell, *Music and Paintings in the National Gallery of Ireland,* Dublin 1985.

Boylan 1968
L. Boylan, 'The Conollys of Castletown. A Family History', *Bulletin of the Irish Georgian Society,* vol. 2, October-December 1968.

Braun 1980
K. Braun, *Alle tot nu toe bekende schilderijen van Jan Steen,* Rotterdam 1980.

Braune 1909
H. Braune, 'Der Name des Meisters der Holzhausen Bildnesse', *Monatshefte für Kunstwissenschaft,* vol. 2, 1909, p. 582.

Bredius 1927
A. Bredius, *Jan Steen,* Amsterdam 1927.

Brière-Misme 1928
C. Brière-Misme, 'Jan Steen' (review of Bredius 1927), *La Revue de L'Art,* vol. 53, May 1928.

Brigstocke 1979
H. Brigstocke, review of 1978 London exhibition, *Arte Lombarda,* no. 51, 1979, pp. 93-97.

Brigstocke 1988
H. Brigstocke, review of Wynne 1986, *Burlington Magazine,* vol. 130, January 1988, pp. 40-41.

Brochhagen and Knüttel 1967
E. Brochhagen and B. Knüttel, *Alte Pinakothek, Munich, Holländische Malerei des 17 Jahrhunderts,* Munich 1967.

Broulhiet 1938
G. Broulhiet, *Meindert Hobbema (1638-1709),* Paris 1938.

Brown 1984
C. Brown, 'The Beit Collection', *Irish Arts Review,* vol. 1, no. 4, Winter 1984, pp. 14-23.

Brown 1966
C. M. Brown, *Lorenzo Costa* (Doctoral Dissertation, Columbia University), 1966.

Brown 1986
J. Brown, *Velázquez,* New Haven and London 1986.

Brücker 1965
W. Brücker, *Conrad Faber von Creuznach,* Frankfurt 1965.

Bruyn 1987
J. Bruyn, 'Towards a Scriptural Reading of Seventeenth-Century Dutch Landscape Painting', in *Masters of 17th Century Dutch Landscape Painting,* Exhibition catalogue, Amsterdam, Boston and Philadelphia 1987.

Buchanan 1824
W. Buchanan, *Memoirs of Painting, with a chronological history of the Importation of Pictures by the Great Masters into England since the French Revolution,* London 1824.

Burger 1865
W. Burger, *Trésors d'Art en Angleterre,* 3rd ed., Paris 1865.

Burke 1976
J. Burke, *English Art 1714-1800,* Oxford 1976.

de Burtin 1808
F.-X. de Burtin, *Traité Théoretique et Pratique,* 2 vols., Brussels 1808.

Busignani 1962
Alberto Busignani, 'Due ritratti fiorentini', *Antichità Viva,* 1962, pp. 15-20.

Cagli and Valcanover 1969
C. Cagli and F. Valcanover, *L'Opera Completa di Tiziano,* Milan 1969.

Calbi and Kelescian 1984
E. Calbi and D. S. Kelescian, *Marcello Oretti e il patrimonio artisticoprivato bolognese,* Bologna 1984.

Camón Aznar 1964
J. Camón Aznar, *Velázquez,* 2 vols., Madrid 1964.

Camón Aznar 1980
J. Camón Aznar, *Francisco de Goya,* 4 vols., Zaragoza 1980.

Campbell 1990
L. Campbell, *Renaissance Portraits: European Portrait Painting in the 14th, 15th and 16th Centuries,* New Haven and London 1990.

Cappelli 1930
A. Cappelli, *Cronologia, Cronografia e Calendario Perpetuo,* 2nd ed., Milan 1930.

Cappi Bentivegna 1962
F. Cappi Bentivegna, *Abbigliamento e costume nella pittura italiana,* 2 vols., Rome 1962.

Chantelou 1885
P. Freart de Chantelou, *Journal de voyage du Cavalier Bernin en France,* ed. Lalanne, 1885, new ed. 1981.

Chimirri and Frangipane 1914
B. Chimirri and A. Frangipane, *Mattia Preti detto Il Cavaliere Calabrese,* Milan 1914.

Christiansen 1992
K. Christiansen, in *Andrea Mantegna,* Exhibition catalogue, Royal Academy, London and Metropolitan Museum of Art, New York 1992.

Clark 1985
A. M. Clark, *Pompeo Batoni. A Complete Catalogue of his Works with an Introductory Text,* ed. E. P. Bowron, Oxford 1985.

Collins Baker 1920
C. H. Collins Baker, 'Syon House and its treasures. Notes on Syon House Pictures, Part II', *The Connoisseur,* vol. 27, 1920, pp. 191-99.

Conisbee 1985
P. Conisbee, *Chardin,* London 1985.

Constans 1980
C. Constans, *Musée National du Chateau de Versailles: Catalogue des Peintures,* Paris 1980.

Conway 1885
W. M. Conway, 'Old Masters at the Royal Academy', *The Academy,* 17 January 1885, pp. 49-51.

Cook 1902
H. Cook, 'Pitture italiane esposte a Burlington House', *L'Arte,* vol. 5, 1902, pp. 114-22.

Cook 1915a
H. Cook, 'Further light on Baldassare d'Este', *Burlington Magazine,* vol. 27, 1915, pp. 98-104.

Cook 1915b
H. Cook, 'More portraits by Sofonisba Anguissola', *Burlington Magazine,* vol. 27, 1915, pp. 228-36.

Cormack 1970
M. Cormack, 'The Ledgers of Sir Joshua Reynolds', Walpole Society, vol. 42, 1968-70, pp. 105-69.

Courthion 1932
P. Courthion, *Claude Gellée,* Paris 1932.

Crelly 1962
W. R. Crelly, *The Paintings of Simon Vouet,* New Haven 1962.

Crelly 1981
W. R. Crelly, 'Two Allegories of the Seasons by Simon Vouet and their Iconography' in *Art, The Ape of Nature, Studies in Honor of H. W. Janson,* New York 1981, pp. 401-24.

Cugini 1939
D. Cugini, *Moroni Pittore,* Bergamo 1939 (reprinted 1978).

Cugini 1953
D. Cugini, 'Rilievi sulla mostra di Palazzo Reale a Milano', *L'Eco di Bergamo,* 23 July 1953, p. 3.

Cuzin 1978
J.-P. Cuzin, 'A Hypothesis concerning the Le Nain Brothers', *Burlington Magazine,* vol. 120, December 1978, pp. 875-76.

Cuzin 1979
J.-P. Cuzin, 'Les frères Le Nain, la part de Mathieu', *Paragone,* no. 349-51, March-May 1979, pp. 58-70.

Cuzin, Vasselin and Thuillier 1983-84
J.-P. Cuzin, M. Vasselin and J. Thuillier, *Hommage à Raphaël: Raphaël et l'art français,* Exhibition catalogue, Grand Palais, Paris 1983-84.

David 1867
J. David, *Notice sur le Marat de Louis David suivie de la liste de ses tableaux dressée par lui-même,* Paris 1867.

David 1880-82
J. David, *Le Peintre Louis David, 1748-1825, I. Souvenirs et documents inédits; II. Suite d'eaux-fortes d'après ses oeuvres gravées par J. L. Jules David son petit-fils,* Paris, vol. 1 1880, vol. 2 1882.

del Caso 1972
J. del Caso, 'Jacques-Louis David and the style *All'antica',* *Burlington Magazine,* vol. 114, October 1972, pp. 686-90.

del Serra 1985
A. del Serra, 'A conversation on painting techniques', *Burlington Magazine,* vol. 127, January 1985, pp. 4-16.

Delogu 1928
G. Delogu, *G. B. Castiglione detto il Grechetto,* Bologna 1928.

Denvir 1950
B. Denvir, *Chardin,* Zurich 1950.

Descamps 1753-64
J. P. Descamps, *La Vie des Peintres Flamands, Allemands et Hollandais,* 4 vols., Paris 1753-64.

Diderot 1781
D. Diderot, *Salons,* ed. J. Seznec and J. Adhémar, 4 vols., Oxford 1957-67.

Dobson 1907
A. Dobson, *William Hogarth,* London 1907 ed.

Donald 1970
A. Donald, 'Some Re-Attributions in the French Collection at Kelvingrove', *Scottish Art Revue,* no. 12, 4, 1970, pp. 11-14, 34.

Doyle 1890
H. Doyle, *Catalogue of the Works of Art in the National Gallery of Ireland,* Dublin 1890.

Dülberg 1990
A. Dülberg, *Privatporträts-Geschichte und Ikonologie einer Gattung im 15 und 16 Jahrhundert,* 2 vols., Berlin 1990.

Duncan 1906-07
E. Duncan, 'The National Gallery of Ireland', *Burlington Magazine,* vol. 10, 1906-07, pp. 7-23.

Dunker and Maillet 1771
Dunker and Maillet, *Réceuil d'éstampes...du Cabinet...du Choiseul,* Paris 1771.

Durantini 1983
M. F. Durantini, *The Child in Seventeenth-Century Dutch Painting,* Dissertation, Ann Arbor 1983.

Duret 1882
T. Duret, 'Une visite aux Galeries Nationales d'Irlande et d'Ecosse', *Gazette des Beaux-Arts,* vol. 25, 1882, pp. 181-85.

Einberg 1989
E. Einberg, 'Venice Fondazione Cini: William Hogarth', review, *Burlington Magazine,* vol. 131, November 1989, pp. 798-99.

Emiliani 1958
A. Emiliani, 'Orazio Gentileschi: nuove proposte per il viaggio marchigiano', *Paragone,* no. 103, 1958, p. 38.

Fahy 1976
E. Fahy, *Some Followers of Domenico Ghirlandaio,* New York 1976.

Félibien 1672-88 and 1725
A. Félibien, *Entretiens sur les vies et sur les ouvrages des plus excellens peintres anciens et modernes,* 5 vols. in 3 parts., Paris 1672-88. Also 1725 edition.

Ferretti 1978
M. Ferretti, 'Di nuovo sul percorso lucchese', *Annali della Scuola Normale di Pisa,* ser. 3, vol. 8, 3, 1978, pp. 1237-51.

Fétis 1878
E. Fétis, *La Galerie du Vicomte du Bus de Gisignies,* Brussels 1878.

Fierens 1933
J. Fierens, *Les Le Nain,* (Art et Artistes français), Paris 1933.

Fiocco 1932
Giuseppe Fiocco, 'Porträts aus der Emilia', *Pantheon,* vol. 9, 1932, pp. 337-43.

Fischel 1935
O. Fischel, 'Art and Theatre', *Burlington Magazine,* vol. 66, January 1935, pp. 4-14.

Fisher 1977
M. R. Fisher, *Titian's Assistants During the Later Years* (Garland Outstanding Dissertations in the Fine Arts), New York and London, 1977.

Friedländer 1902
M. J. Friedländer, 'Die Leihausstellung der Royal Academy von 1902', *Repertorium fur Kunstwissenschaft,* vol. 25, 1902, pp. 142-47.

Friedländer 1913
M. J. Friedländer, 'Conrad Faber: Painter of the Patricians of Frankfort in the second quarter of the sixteenth century', *Art in America,* vol. 1, no. 3, July 1913, p. 143ff.

Friedlaender 1914
W. Friedlaender, *Nicolas Poussin, Die Entwicklung seiner Kunst,* Munich 1914.

Friedlaender 1965
W. Friedlaender, *Nicolas Poussin,* Paris 1965.

Friedlaender and Blunt 1939
W. Friedlaender and A. Blunt, *The Drawings of Nicolas Poussin, a catalogue raisonné,* London 1939.

Furst 1911
H. E. A. Furst, *Chardin,* London 1911.

Galetti and Camesasca 1951
U. Galetti and E. Camesasca, *Enciclopedia della Pittura Italiana,* Milan 1951.

Gamba 1934
C. Gamba, 'Moroni: Giovan Battista', *Enciclopedia Italiana,* vol. 23, Rome 1934.

Gamba 1958
F. Gamba, *Filippino Lippi nella storia della critica,* Florence 1958.

Garstang 1987
D. Garstang, review of Wynne 1986, *Apollo,* vol. 125, Feb. 1987, p. 152.

Gaskell 1982
L. Gaskell, 'Transformations of Cervantes's *La Gitanilla* in Dutch Art', *Journal of the Warburg and Courtauld Institutes,* vol. 45, 1982, pp. 263-70.

Gassier 1971
P. Gassier and J. Wilson, *The Life and Complete Work of Goya,* New York, 1971.

Gaya Nuño 1953
J. A. Gaya Nuño, 'Despues de Justi. Medio siglo de estudios velazquistas', App. to Spanish edition of Justi, *Velázquez y su siglo,* Madrid 1953.

Gaya Nuño 1958
A. Gaya Nuño, *La Pintura Española fuera de Espana,* Madrid 1958.

van Gelder 1926
J. G. van Gelder, 'Een Vroeg Werk van Jan Steen', *Oud Holland,* vol. 43, 1926.

Gemäldegalerie 1979
Gemäldegalerie Alte Meister Dresden, Dresden 1979.

Georgian Soc. Records 1913
The Georgian Society Records of Eighteenth-Century Domestic Architecture and Decoration in Ireland, vol. 5, Dublin 1913.

Gérard 1852-7
H. Gérard, *L'Oeuvre du Baron Gérard 1789-1836. Gravures à l'eau forte,* 3 vols., Paris 1852-57.

Gérard 1886
H. Gérard, ed. *Lettres addressées au Baron François Gérard peintre d'histoire par les artistes et les personnages célèbres de son temps. Deuxième édition publiée par le Baron Gérard son nevue et precedée d'une notice sur la vie et les oeuvres de François Gérard et d'un récit d'Alexandre Gérard, son frère,* 2 vols., Paris 1886.

Gerstenberg 1957
K. Gerstenberg, *Velásquez,* Berlin 1957.

Ginnings 1970
R. J. Ginnings, *The Art of Jan Baptist Weenix and Jan Weenix,* Dissertation, University of Delaware 1970.

Glendinning 1980
N. Glendinning, 'Goya's Patrons', *Apollo,* vol. 114, October 1981, pp. 236-47.

Gore 1955
St. John Gore, 'An "Ecce Homo" in Dublin', *Burlington Magazine,* vol. 97, July 1955, pp. 218-19.

Gotker 1964
H. Gotker, 'Beitrag zur Baugeschichte der Burg Bentheim', *Jahrbuch des Heimatvereins der Grafschaft Bentheim,* 1964.

Gould 1978
C. Gould, 'G. B. Moroni and the Genre Portrait in the Cinquecento', *Apollo,* vol. 108, November 1978, pp. 316-21.

Graff 1912
W. Graff, 'Ein Familienbildnis des Baldassare Estense in der Alten Pinakothek', *Münchener Jahrbuch der Bildenden Kunst,* vol. 7, 1912, pp. 207-24.

Grautoff 1914
O. Grautoff, *Nicolas Poussin: sein Werk und sein Leben,* 2 vols., London 1914.

Graves and Cronin 1899-1901
A. Graves and W. Cronin, *History of the Works of Sir Joshua Reynolds,* 4 vols., London 1899-1901.

Gregori and Rossi 1979
M. Gregori and F. Rossi, 'Giovan Battista Moroni', *I Pittori Bergamaschi dal XIII al XIX secolo: Il Cinquecento,* III, Bergamo 1979, pp. 95-377 (also printed separately, as monograph).

Greindl 1956 and 1983
E. Greindl, *Les Peintres Flamands de Nature Morte au XVIIe Siècle,* Brussels 1956; revised ed. Sterrebeek 1983.

Grimm 1988
C. Grimm, *Stilleben - Die Nederlandischen und Deutschen Meister,* Stuttgart 1988.

de Groot 1952
C. W. de Groot, *Jan Steen: beeld en woord,* Utrecht and Nijmegen 1952.

Gudiol 1971
J. Gudiol, *Goya,* 4 vols., Barcelona 1971 (English translation of Spanish ed., 1971).

Gudlaagsson 1945
Gudlaagsson, *De komedianten bij Jan Steen en zijn tijdegenoten,* The Hague 1945.

Guinard 1960
P. Guinard, *Zurbarán et les peintres espagñols de la vie monastique,* Paris 1960.

Guinness and Ryan 1971
D. Guinness and W. Ryan, *Irish Houses and Castles,* London 1971.

Habich 1908-09
G. Habich, 'Anton Hundertpfundt und Matthias Zasinger', *Mitteilungen der Bayerischen Numismatischen Gesellschaft,* vols. 36, 37, 1908-09, p. 57.

Hagels 1968
H. Hagels, 'Die Gemälde der niederlandischen Maler Jacob van Ruisdael vom Schloss Bentheim in Verhaltnis zur Natur des Bentheimer Landes', *Jahrbuch des Heimatvereins der Grafschaft Bentheim,* 1968.

Haillet de Couronne 1854
Haillet de Couronne, 'Eloge de M. Chardin', *Mémoires inédits,* published by Dussieux, Soulie et al., vol. 2, Paris 1854, pp. 428-41.

Hairs 1965 and 1985
M.-L. Hairs, *Les Peintres Flamandes de Fleurs au XVIIe Siècle,* Paris and Brussels 1965, 2nd ed.; *The Flemish Flower Painters in the XVIIth Century,* Brussels 1985, English ed.

Haraszti-Takács 1973
M. Haraszti-Takács, 'Quelques problèmes des bodegones de Velázquez', *Bulletin du Musée Hongrois des Beaux-Arts,* no. 41, 1973, pp. 21-48.

Haraszti-Takács 1983
M. Haraszti-Takács, *Spanish Genre Painting in the Seventeenth Century,* Budapest 1983.

Harris 1982
E. Harris, *Velázquez,* Oxford 1982.

Hayes 1970
J. Hayes, *The Drawings of Thomas Gainsborough,* New Haven and London 1970.

Hayes 1975
J. Hayes, *Gainsborough: Paintings and Drawings,* London 1975.

Hayes 1982
J. Hayes, *The Landscape Paintings of Thomas Gainsborough,* 2 vols., London 1982.

Heinemann 1980
F. Heinemann, 'La Bottega di Tiziano', *Tiziano e Venezia: Convegno Internazionale di Studi* (Venice 1976), Vicenza 1980, p. 440.

Heinzle 1953
E. Heinzle, *Wolf Huber um 1485-1553,* Innsbruck 1953.

Hempel 1965
E. Hempel, *Baroque Art and Architecture in Central Europe,* Harmondsworth 1965.

Henkell 1939
M.D. Henkell, 'Dirck Maes' in Thieme and Becker 1907-50, vol. 23, pp. 544-45.

Heppner 1939-40
A. Heppner, 'The popular theatre of the Rederijkers in the works of Jan Steen and his contemporaries', *Journal of the Warburg and Courtauld Institutes,* vol. 3, 1939-40.

Hibbard 1974
H. Hibbard, *Poussin: The Holy Family on the Steps,* London 1974.

Hill 1951
J. Hill, 'Iconografia di Angelo Poliziano', *Rinascimento,* 1951, pp. 261-92.

Hoet 1752
G. Hoet, *Catalogus of Maamlyst van schilderyen,* 3 vols. in 2 parts, The Hague 1752.

Hofstede de Groot 1908-27
C. Hofstede de Groot, *A Catalogue Raisonné of the Works of the Most Eminent Dutch Painters of the Seventeenth Century,* translated by E. G. Hawke, 8 vols., London 1908-27.

Holmes 1909
C. J. Holmes, 'Notes on the Chronology of Jan Steen', *Burlington Magazine,* vol. 15, July 1909, pp. 243-44.

Hope 1980
C. Hope, *Titian,* London 1980.

Houbraken 1718-21
A. Houbraken, *De Groote Schouburgh der Nederlantsche Konstschilders en Schilderessen,* 3 vols., Amsterdam 1718-21.

Howard 1975
S. Howard, *Sacrifice of the Hero: The Roman Years, a Classical Frieze by Jacques-Louis David,* Sacramento 1975.

Hubert 1976
Nicole Hubert, 'À propos de quelques toilettes de Julie et de Desirée Clary', *Bulletin du Musée Bernadotte,* Pau, no. 21, December 1976, pp. 33-36.

Hugelshofer 1939a
W. Hugelshofer, 'Gemälde Deutscher Meister in der National Gallery of Ireland in Dublin', *Pantheon,* vol. 23, 1939, pp. 18-24.

Hugelshofer 1939b
W. Hugelshofer, 'Wolf Huber als Bildnismaler', *Pantheon,* vol. 23, 1939, pp. 230-36.

Ionescu 1960
T. Ionescu, 'Un "Ecce Homo" di Tiziano al Museo Brukenthal', *Paragone,* no. 129, 1960, pp. 38-45.

Ionescu 1961
T. Ionescu, 'Un tablou de Tiziano la Sibiu', *Omagiu lui George Oprescu,* Bucharest 1961, pp. 273-82.

Isarlo 1938
G. Isarlo, 'Les trois Le Nain et leur suite', *La Renaissance,* no. 1, March 1938, pp. 1-58.

Jamot 1923
P. Jamot, 'Essai de Chronologie des oeuvres des frères Le Nain', *Gazette des Beaux-Arts,* March 1923, pp. 157-66.

Jamot 1929
P. Jamot, *Les Le Nain, 'Les Grands Artistes, leur vie, leur oeuvre',* Paris 1929.

Johnson 1986
E. D. H. Johnson, *Painters of the British Social Scene from Hogarth to Sickert,* London 1986.

de Jongh 1972-73
E. de Jongh, review of Niemeijer, 1973, *Simiolus* vol. 7, 1974, pp. 76-80.

Justi 1953
Justi, *Velázquez y su siglo,* Madrid 1953.

Kalnein and Levey 1972
W. G. Kalnein and M. Levey, *Art and Architecture of the Eighteenth Century in France,* Harmondsworth 1972.

Keaveney et al 1990
R. Keaveney, M. Wynne, A. Le Harivel and F. Croke, *National Gallery of Ireland,* London 1990.

Keller 1979
A. M. Keller, 'The Long Gallery at Castletown House', *Bulletin of the Irish Georgian Society,* vol. 22, 1979, pp. 1-53.

Kirschenbaum 1977
B. D. Kirschenbaum, *The Religious and Historical Paintings of Jan Steen,* Oxford 1977.

Kitson 1962
M. Kitson in *L'ideale classico del seicento in Italia e la pittura di paesaggio,* Exhibition catalogue, Palazzo dell'Archiginnasio, Bologna.

Kitson 1978
M. Kitson, *Claude Lorrain: Liber Veritatis,* London 1978.

Kitson 1990
M. Kitson in *Claude to Corot. The Development of Landscape Painting in France,* Exhibition catalogue, (ed. A. Wintermule), Colnaghi, New York 1990, pp.30-31.

Knoef 1947a
J. Knoef, *Cornelis Troost,* Amsterdam 1947.

Knoef 1947b
J. Knoef, 'Een portret van Tonneman?', *Kunsthistorische mededelingen,* vol. 2, 1947, p. 14.

Korn 1978
U. D. Korn, 'Ruisdael in Steinfurt', *Westfalen: Hefte für Geschichte, Kunst und Volkskunde,* vol. 56, 1978.

Kozakiewicz 1972
S. Kozakiewicz, *Bernardo Bellotto,* 2 vols., Recklinghausen 1972.

Kreplin 1942
B. C. Kreplin, 'Jan Baptist Weenix', in Thieme and Becker 1907-50, vol. 35, pp. 246-47.

Kristeller 1901
P. Kristeller, *Andrea Mantegna,* London, New York and Bombay 1901.

Kühnel-Kunze 1962
I. Kühnel-Kunze, 'Zur Bildenkunst der Sofonisba Anguissola und Lucia Anguissola', *Pantheon,* vol. 20, 1962, pp. 83-96.

Lafuente Ferrari 1943
E. Lafuente Ferrari, *Velázquez,* London and New York 1943.

Lafuente Ferrari 1944
E. Lafuente Ferrari, 'Nuevas notas sobre Escalante', *Arte Espanol,* vol. 15, 1944, pp. 1-9.

Laroque 1872
L. de Laroque, *Biographie Montpellieraine, Peintres, Sculptures, et Architectes,* Montpellier 1872.

Latreille 1989
A. Latreille, *1789: French Art During the Revolution,* Exhibition catalogue, Colnaghi, New York 1989.

Laveissière 1985
S. Laveissière, *Le Classicisme Français. Masterpieces of seventeenth century painting,* Exhibition catalogue, National Gallery of Ireland, Dublin 1985.

Laver 1969
J. A. Laver, *A Concise History of Fashion,* London 1969.

Leahy 1968
Fr. Timothy Leahy, *Beyond Tomorrow,* 4th ed., Dublin 1968.

Lenormant 1847
C. Lenormant, *François Gérard, peintre d'histoire, essai de biographie et de critique,* 2nd ed., Paris 1847.

Lerndorff 1933
G. Lerndorff, *Moroni der Porträt-Maler von Bergamo,* Winterthur 1933.

Lerndorff 1939
G. Lerndorff, *Giovanni Battista Moroni, il ritrattista bergamasco,* Bergamo 1939 (reprinted 1978).

von Lersner 1706
A. A. von Lersner, *Chronica der Weit-Beruhmten Freyen Reichs-Wahl und Handels-Staat Frankfort-am-Main,* Frankfurt 1706.

Leslie and Taylor 1865
C. R. Leslie and T. Taylor, *The Life and Times of Sir Joshua Reynolds with Notices of some of his Contemporaries,* 2 vols., London 1865.

Levey 1986
M. Levey, *Giambattista Tiepolo,* New Haven and London 1986.

Lewis 1837
S. Lewis, *A Topographical Dictionary of Ireland,* 2 vols., London 1837.

Lightbown 1978
R. Lightbown, *Sandro Botticelli,* 2 vols., London 1978.

Lightbown 1986
R. Lightbown, *Mantegna: with a complete catalogue of the paintings and drawings and prints,* Oxford 1986.

Lindsay 1977
J. Lindsay, *Hogarth, his Art and his World,* London 1977.

Lindsay 1981
J. Lindsay, *Thomas Gainsborough: his Life and Art,* London 1981.

Longhi 1934
R. Longhi, *Officina Ferrarese,* Rome 1934.

López-Rey 1963
J. López-Rey, *Velázquez: a catalogue raisonné of his oeuvre,* London 1963.

López-Rey 1968
J. López-Rey, *Velázquez's Work and World,* London 1968.

López-Rey 1979
J. López-Rey, *Velázquez: The Artist as a Maker. With a Catalogue Raisonné of his extant works,* Lausanne and Paris 1979.

Luna 1989
J. J. Luna, *Summa Artis vol. 33: Pintura Británica (1500-1820),* Madrid 1989.

MacGreevy 1945
T. MacGreevy, *Pictures in the Irish National Gallery,* London 1945.

MacGreevy 1956
T. MacGreevy, *National Gallery of Ireland, Catalogue of Pictures of the Italian Schools,* Dublin 1956.

MacGreevy 1964
T. MacGreevy, *National Gallery of Ireland, Concise catalogue of the oil paintings,* Dublin 1964.

MacGregor 1979
N. MacGregor, 'The Le Nain Brothers and Changes in French Rural Life', *Art History,* vol. 2, no. 4, December 1979, pp. 401-12.

Magne 1914
E. Magne, *Nicolas Poussin, premier peintre du roi, 1594-1665,* Brussels and Paris 1914.

Mahon 1960
D. Mahon, 'Poussin's early development: an alternative hypothesis', *Burlington Magazine,* vol. 102, July 1960, pp. 288-305.

Mahon 1961
D. Mahon, 'Réflexions sur les paysages de Poussin', *Art de France,* 1, 1961, pp. 119ff.

Mahon 1962
'Poussiniana: afterthoughts arising from the exhibition', *Gazette des Beaux-Arts,* July-Aug 1962, pp. 1-135.

Mandel 1967
G. Mandel, *L'Opera Completa di Hogarth,* Milan 1967.

Mariette 1853-62
P.-J. Mariette, *Abécédario,* published by Chennevières and Montaiglon, Archives de L'Art Français, 1853-62.

van Marle 1923-38
R. van Marle, *Development of the Italian Schools of Painting,* 19 vols., The Hague 1923-38.

Martin 1909
W. Martin, 'L'Exposition Jan Steen à Londres', *L'Art flamande et hollandais,* vol. 12, 1909.

Martin 1927-28
W. Martin, 'Neues über Jan Steen', *Zeitschrift für bilddende Kunst,* vol. 61, 1927-28.

Martin 1954
W. Martin, *Jan Steen,* Amsterdam 1954.

Maschmayer 1978
D. Maschmayer, 'Jacob Isaackszoon van Ruisdael und Meindert Hobbema malen Motive aus der Grafschaft Bentheim und ihrer Umgelring', *Jahrbuch das Heimatvereins der Grafschaft Bentheim, Das Bentheimer Land,* vol. 92, 1978.

Mather 1923
F. J. Mather, *A History of Italian Painting,* New York 1923.

Matteoli 1990
A. Matteoli, *La problematica sui fratelli Le Nain e loro cerchia,* Pisa 1990.

Mauritshuis 1980
Mauritshuis Landschappen 17de Eeuw, The Hague 1980.

Mayer 1922
A. L. Mayer, 'Some unknown works by Zurbarán', *Burlington Magazine,* vol. 41, July 1922, p. 42.

Mayer 1924
A. L. Mayer, *Francisco de Goya,* London and Toronto 1924.

Mayer 1927
A. L. Mayer, 'Das Original der "Kuchenmagd" von Velázquez', *Der Cicerone,* Sept.-Dec. 1927, pp. 562-63.

Mayer 1936
A. L. Mayer, *Velázquez: a Catalogue Raisonné of the Pictures and Drawings,* London 1936.

Mazza 1939
E. Mazza, 'Giambattista Moroni', *Giambattista Moroni Pittore,* Albino 1939, p. 30.

Menpes and Greig 1909
M. Menpes and J. Greig, *Gainsborough,* London 1909.

Meroni 1971
U. Meroni, ed., *Fonti per la storia della Pittura. I Serie Documentaria. Lettere e altri documenti informo alla Storia della Pittura,* Genoa 1971.

Merten 1928
H. Merten, *Giovanni Battista Moroni. Des Meisters Gemälde und Zeichnungen,* Marburg 1928.

Michel 1910
E. Michel, *Great Masters of Landscape Painting,* London 1910.

Milford 1932
H. Milford, *Commemorative Catalogue of the Exhibition of French Art, 1200-1900,* Royal Academy, London 1932.

Millar 1949
O. Millar, *Thomas Gainsborough,* London 1949.

Milltown 1863
A Catalogue of Pictures, belonging to the Earl of Milltown, at Russborough, Dublin 1863.

de Mirimonde 1971
A. P. de Mirimonde, 'Musique et symbolisme chez Jan Davidszoon de Heem, Cornelis Janszoon et Jan II Janszoon de Heem', *Jaarboek van het Koninklijk Museum voor Schone Kunsten van Antwerpen 1970,* 1971, pp. 241-96.

Molajoli 1974
R. Molajoli, *L'Opera Completa di Cosmè Tura e i grandi pittori ferraresi del suo tempo: Francesco del Cossa, Ercole de'Roberti,* Milan 1974.

Morassi 1962
A. Morassi, *A Complete Catalogue of the Paintings of G. B. Tiepolo,* London 1962.

Mortari 1966
L. Mortari, *Bernardo Strozzi,* Rome 1966.

Mulcahy 1984
R. Mulcahy, 'Spanish Masterpieces in Dublin', *Irish Arts Review,* vol. 1, no. 3, Autumn 1984, pp. 29-36.

Mulcahy 1988
R. Mulcahy, *Spanish Paintings in the National Gallery of Ireland,* Dublin 1988.

Natale 1980
M. Natale, 'Note sulla pittura lucchese alla fine del quattrocento', *J. Paul Getty Museum Journal,* vol. 8, 1980, pp. 35-62.

Neale 1826
J. P. Neale, *Views of the Seats of Noblemen and Gentlemen in the United Kingdom,* 2nd series, 3 vols., London 1826.

Nichols 1833
J. B. Nichols, *Anecdotes of William Hogarth,* London 1833.

Nichols et al. 1781 and 1782
J. B. Nichols et al., *Biographical Anecdotes of William Hogarth,* London 1781, 2nd ed. London 1782.

Nichols and Steevens 1808-17
J. B. Nichols and G. Steevens, *The Genuine Works of William Hogarth,* 3 vols., London 1808-17.

Niemeijer 1973
J. W. Niemeijer, *Cornelis Troost 1696-1750,* Assen 1973.

Oberhuber 1966
K. Oberhuber, 'Eine unbekannte Zeichnung Raffaels in den Uffizien', *Mitteilungen des kunsthistorischen Instituts in Florenz,* 12, 1966, pp. 225-44.

Oberhuber 1988
K. Oberhuber, *Poussin. The Early Years in Rome,* Exhibition catalogue (Fort Worth), New York 1988.

Oberhuber, Levinson and Sheehan 1973
K. Oberhuber, J. A. Levinson and J. L. Sheehan, *Early Italian Engravings from the National Gallery of Art,* Exhibition catalogue, National Gallery of Art, Washington 1973.

Oldfield 1987
D. Oldfield, *German Paintings in the National Gallery of Ireland,* Dublin 1987.

Oliver 1896
V. L. Oliver, *The History of the Island of Antigua,* 2 vols., London 1896.

Ortega y Gasset 1954
J. Ortega y Gasset, *Velázquez,* Zurich 1954.

Ortiz et al 1989
A. D. Ortiz, A.E. Pérèz Sánchez and J. Gállego, *Velázquez,* New York 1989.

Ortolani 1941
S. Ortolani, *Cosmè Tura, Francesco del Cossa, Ercole de'Roberti,* Milan 1941.

von der Osten and Vey 1969
G. von der Osten and H. Vey, *Painting and Sculpture in Germany and the Netherlands 1500-1600,* Harmondsworth 1969.

Paccagnini 1961
G. Paccagnini, *Andrea Mantegna,* Exhibition catalogue, Palazzo Ducale, Mantua 1961.

Pallucchini 1968
A. Pallucchini, *L'Opera Completa di Giambattista Tiepolo,* Milan 1968.

Pallucchini 1969
R. Pallucchini, *Tiziano,* Florence 1969.

Pantorba 1955
B. Pantorba, *La vida y la obra de Velázquez,* Madrid 1955.

Pascal and Gaucheron 1931
A. Pascal and R. Gaucheron, *Documents sur l'oeuvre et la vie de Chardin,* Paris 1931.

Pattison 1884
Mrs Mark Pattison (E. F. S. Dilke), *Claude Lorrain, sa vie et ses oeuvres, d'après des documents inédits,* Paris 1884.

Paulson 1971
R. Paulson, *Hogarth: His Life, Art and Times,* 2 vols., New Haven and London 1971.

Penny and Mannings 1986
N. Penny and D. Mannings, 'Arising from the Reynolds Exhibition', *Burlington Magazine,* vol. 128, October 1986, pp. 760-62.

Pératé 1909-10
A. Pératé, 'Les esquisses de Gérard', *L'Art et les Artistes,* vol. 10, 1909-10, pp. 7ff.

Percy 1971
A. Percy, in *Giovanni Benedetto Castiglione,* Exhibition catalogue, Philadelphia Museum of Art 1971.

Pérèz Sánchez 1980
A. E. Pérèz Sánchez, 'La Obra de Diego Polo, Imitador Espanol de Tiziano', *Tiziano e Venezia: Convegna Internazionale di Studi* (Venice, 1976), Vicenza 1980.

Pigler 1974
A. Pigler, *Barockthemen,* 3 vols., Budapest 1974.

Pignatti 1981
T. Pignatti, *Tiziano,* 2 vols., 1981.

Pilon 1909
E. Pilon, *Chardin,* Paris 1909, reprinted 1941.

Piper 1975
D. Piper, ed., *The Genius of British Painting,* London 1975.

Potterton 1981
H. Potterton (ed.), *Illustrated Summary Catalogue of Paintings, National Gallery of Ireland,* Dublin 1981.

Potterton 1982
H. Potterton, 'Recently cleaned Dutch pictures in the National Gallery of Ireland', *Apollo,* vol. 115, 1982, pp. 104-07.

Potterton 1986
H. Potterton, *Dutch Seventeenth- and Eighteenth-Century Paintings in the National Gallery of Ireland, a complete catalogue,* Dublin 1986.

Powerscourt 1903
Viscount Powerscourt, *A Description and History of Powerscourt,* London 1903.

Praz 1971
M. Praz, *Conversation Pieces. A Survey of the Informal Group Portrait in Europe and America,* London 1971.

Public Advertiser 1774
Public Advertiser, London 1774.

Ragghianti 1960
C. L. Ragghianti, 'Filippino Lippi a Lucca: l'altare Magrini, nuovi problemi e nuove soluzione', *Critica d'Arte,* no. 7, 1960, pp. 1-56.

Rearick 1980
W. R. Rearick, 'Tiziano e Jacopo Bassano', *Tiziano e Venezia: Convegno Internazionale di Studi* (Venice, 1976), Vicenza 1980.

Reau 1955-59
L. Reau, *Iconographie de L'Art Chrétien,* 3 tomes in 6 vols., Paris 1955-59.

Richter 1884
J. P. Richter, 'The Italian Pictures at Burlington House', *The Academy,* XXV, 19 January 1884, pp. 50-51.

de Ridder 1932
A. de Ridder, *J. B. Siméon Chardin,* Paris 1932.

Roethlisberger 1960
M. Roethlisberger, 'The Subjects of Claude Lorrain's Paintings', *Gazette des Beaux-Arts,* April 1960, pp. 209-24.

Roethlisberger 1968
M. Roethlisberger, *Claude Lorrain. The Drawings,* 2 vols., Berkeley - Los Angeles 1968.

Roethlisberger 1977
M. Roethlisberger, *Tout l'oeuvre peint de Claude Lorrain,* assisted by D. Cecchi, Paris 1977.

Roethlisberger 1979
M. Roethlisberger, *Claude Lorrain, The Paintings. A Critical Catalogue,* 2 vols., 2nd ed. New York 1979.

Roodenbeke 1981
M.- T. de Roodenbeke, 'Précisions nouvelles sur les oeuvres des Le Nain', *Bulletin de la Societé de l'Histoire de l'Art Français,* 1979 (1981), pp. 100-10.

Rose 1977
P. Rose, *Wolf Huber Studies. Aspects of Renaissance Thought and Practice in Danube School Painting,* New York and London 1977.

Rosenberg 1927
J. Rosenberg, 'Meindert Hobbema', *Jahrbuch der Preussischen Kunstsammlungen,* vol. 48, 1927.

Rosenberg 1928
J. Rosenberg, *Jacob von Ruisdael,* Berlin 1928.

Rosenberg 1970
P. Rosenberg, 'Twenty French Drawings in Sacramento', *Master Drawings,* vol. 8, no. 1, Spring 1970, pp. 31-39.

Rosenberg 1972-73
P. Rosenberg, *French Master Drawings of the 17th and 18th Centuries in North American Collections,* Exhibition catalogue, Art Gallery of Toronto, 1972-73.

Rosenberg 1973
P. Rosenberg, 'Designi néo-classici françesi al Louvre', *Arte Illustrata,* 6, no. 52, February 1973.

Rosenberg 1977-78
P. Rosenberg, *Nicolas Poussin 1594-1665,* Exhibition catalogue, Academia di Francia a Roma, Villa Medici, Rome 1977-78.

Rosenberg 1979a
P. Rosenberg, *Chardin 1699-1779,* Exhibition catalogue, English translation, Cleveland 1979.

Rosenberg 1979b
P. Rosenberg, 'L'exposition Le Nain: une proposition', *Revue de l'Art,* 1979, pp. 91-100.

Rosenberg 1982
P. Rosenberg, *France in the Golden Age. Seventeenth-Century French Paintings in American Collections,* Exhibition catalogue, English ed., Metropolitan Museum of Art, New York 1982.

Rosenberg 1983a
P. Rosenberg, *L'opera completa de Chardin,* Milan 1983.

Rosenberg 1983b
P. Rosenberg, *Chardin: New Thoughts, The Franklin D. Murphy Lectures I,* Helen Foresman Spenser Museum of Art, University of Kansas 1983.

Rosenberg, Slive and ter Kuile 1966
J. Rosenberg, S. Slive and E. H. ter Kuile, *Dutch Art and Architecture 1600-1800,* Harmondsworth 1966.

Rosenberg and Stewart 1987
P. Rosenberg and M. C. Stewart, *French Paintings 1500-1825, The Fine Arts Museums of San Francisco,* San Francisco 1987.

Rosenblum 1973
R. Rosenblum, 'David's Funeral of Patroclus', *Burlington Magazine,* vol. 115, September 1973, pp. 567-76.

Rosenblum 1974-75
R. Rosenblum, in *De David à Delacroix. La peinture française de 1774 à 1830,* Exhibition catalogue, Grand Palais, Paris; Museum of Art, Detroit; Metropolitan Museum of Art, New York, 1974-75.

Rosenblum 1991
R. Rosenblum, 'The fall and rise of Jacques-Louis David in Dublin' in *Art is my life. A Tribute to James White* (ed. B.P. Kennedy), Dublin 1991, pp. 167-71.

Rossi 1930
F. Rossi, 'Baldassare d'Este', *Enciclopedia Italiana,* vol. 5, p. 941.

Röttgen 1977
S. Röttgen, 'Mengs, Alessandro Albani und Wincklemann - Idee und Gestalt des Parnass in der Villa Albani', *Storia dell'Arte,* 30-31, May-December 1977.

Rowan 1991
A. Rowan, 'The Irish Claudes', in *Art is my life. A Tribute to James White* (ed. B.P. Kennedy), Dublin 1991, pp. 173-83.

Royal Academy 1935
Commemorative Catalogue of the Exhibition of British Art, 1934, Oxford 1935.

Russell 1978
F. Russell, 'The British Portraits of A. R. Mengs', *National Trust Studies 1978,* London 1979.

Russell 1982
F. Russell, 'A list of Pompeo Batoni's British Sitters', in *Pompeo Batoni and his British Patrons,* Exhibition catalogue, (ed. E.P. Bowron), Kenwood, London 1982, pp. 90-94.

Russell 1982
H. D. Russell, *Claude Lorrain 1600-1682,* Exhibition catalogue, National Gallery of Art, Washington 1982.

de Saint Gelais 1727
Du Bois de Saint Gelais, *Description des Tableaux du Palais Royal,* Paris 1727.

Salmi 1957 and 1963
M. Salmi, *Cosmè Tura,* Milan 1957. 2nd edition 1963.

Salomon 1987
N. Salomon, 'Jan Steen's Formulation of the Dissolute Household, Sources and Meanings', *Holländische Genremalerei im 17. Jahrhundert,* Symposium Berlin 1984, in *Jahrbuch Preussischer Kulturbesitz,* Sonderband 4, 1987, pp. 315-45.

von Sandrart 1675-79
J. von Sandrart, *Teutsche Academie,* Nurnberg, 1675-79. English translation in Roethlisberger 1979, pp. 47-52.

Schleier 1962
E. Schleier, 'An Unknown Altarpiece by Orazio Gentileschi', *Burlington Magazine,* vol. 104, October 1962, pp. 432-36.

Schloss 1983
C. Schloss, 'The early Italianate Genre Paintings of Jan Weenix, 1642-1719', *Oud Holland,* vol. 97, no. 2, 1983, pp. 69-97.

Schmidt-Degener and van Gelder 1927
F. Schmidt-Degener and H. E. van Gelder, *Viertig meesterwerken van Jan Steen,* Amsterdam 1927.

Schnapper 1989-90
A. Schnapper et al., *Jacques-Louis David 1748-1825,* Exhibition catalogue, Grand Palais, Paris 1989-90.

Schneider 1990
C. P. Schneider, *Rembrandt's Landscapes,* New Haven and London 1990.

Segal 1988-89
S. Segal in *A Prosperous Past–the Sumptuous Still Life in the Netherlands,* Exhibition catalogue, Stedelijk Museum, Delft, Fogg Art Museum, Cambridge and Fort Worth 1988-89.

Sérullaz 1972
A. Sérullaz, *Dessins français de 1750 à 1825. Le néo-classicisme,* Exhibition catalogue, Musée du Louvre, Cabinet des Dessins, 1972.

Sérullaz 1974-75
A. Sérullaz, in *Le Néo-classicisme français. Dessins des musées de province,* Exhibition catalogue, Paris 1974-75.

Sitwell 1936
S. Sitwell, *Conversation Pieces,* London 1936.

Slive 1981-82
S. Slive, *Jacob van Ruisdael,* Exhibition catalogue, Mauritshuis, The Hague; Fogg Art Museum, Harvard 1981-82.

Smith 1829-42
J. Smith, *A catalogue raisonné of the works of the most eminent Dutch, Flemish and French painters,* 9 vols., London 1829-42.

Smith 1981
A. Smith, *Second Sight: Mantegna: Samson and Delilah. Degas: Beach Scene,* Exhibition catalogue, National Gallery, London, 1981.

Soria 1949
M. S. Soria, 'Christ in the house of Mary and Martha' in 'An unknown early painting by Velazquez', *Burlington Magazine,* vol. 91, May 1949, pp. 125-28.

Spinelli 1978
D. Spinelli, 'Trento lo scopri primo di Bergamo', *L'Eco di Bergamo,* 15 February 1978, p. 3.

Staring 1956
A. Staring, *De Hollanders thuis,* The Hague 1956.

Stechow 1928-29
W. Stechow, 'Bermerkungen zu Jan Steens kunstlerischer Entwicklung', *Zeitschrift für bildende Kunst,* vol. 62, 1928-29.

Stechow 1972
W. Stechow, 'Jan Steen's representations of the Marriage in Cana', *Nederlands Kunsthistorisch Jaarboek,* vol. 23, 1972.

Steegman 1946
J. Steegman, 'Some English Portraits by Pompeo Batoni', *Burlington Magazine,* vol. 88, March 1946, pp. 55-63.

Strutt 1827
A Catalogue of Paintings, Drawings, etc. in the collection of Joseph Strutt, Derby, Derby 1827.

Stutzel 1911
T. Stutzel, 'Ein Altbayerisches Munzmeistergeschlecht', *Altbayerische Monatsschrift,* vol. 10, 1911, pp. 27-31.

Sumowski 1983-
W. Sumowski, *Gemälde der Rembrandt-Schuler,* 4 vols., Landau 1983-

Sutton 1987
P. C. Sutton et al., *Masters of Seventeenth-Century Dutch Landscape Painting,* Exhibition catalogue, Rijksmuseum, Amsterdam; Museum of Fine Arts, Boston; Philadelphia Museum of Arts 1987.

Sutton 1990
P. C. Sutton, *Northern European Paintings in the Philadelphia Museum of Art: From the Sixteenth through the Nineteenth Century,* Philadelphia 1990.

Sutton 1992
P. C. Sutton, *Dutch and Flemish Seventeenth-Century Paintings. The Harold Samuel Collection,* Cambridge University Press 1992.

Taschetta 1959
C. F. Taschetta, *Mattia Preti. Contributi alla conoscenza del Cavalier Calabrese,* Brindisi n.d., but 1959.

Thieme and Becker 1907-50
U. Thieme and F. Becker, eds., *Algemeines Lexikon der bildenden Künstler von der Antike bis zur Gegenwart,* 37 vols., Leipzig 1907-50.

Thuillier 1960
J. Thuillier, 'Pour un corpus Pussinianum', *Actes du Colloque International Nicolas Poussin,* Paris 1960, vol. 2, pp. 49-238.

Thuillier 1961
J. Thuillier, 'Les frères Le Nain: une nouvelle oeuvre religieuse', *Art de France,* 1961, pp. 327-28.

Thuillier 1974
J. Thuillier, *L'opera completa di Poussin,* Milan 1974.

Thuillier 1978
J. Thuillier, *Les Frères Le Nain,* Exhibition catalogue, Grand Palais, Paris 1978.

Thuillier 1990-91
J. Thuillier, *Vouet,* Exhibition catalogue, Grand Palais, Paris 1990-91.

Thuillier and Mignot 1978
J. Thuillier and C. Mignot, 'Collectionneur et peintre au XVIIe siècle: Pointel et Poussin', *Revue de l'Art,* no. 39, 1978, pp. 48-49.

Torriti 1967
P. Torriti, *La Galleria del Palazzo Durazzo Pallavicini a Genova,* Genoa 1967.

Trapier 1948
E. du Gue Trapier, *Velázquez,* New York 1948.

Vaillat and de Limay 1923
L. Vaillat and P. Ratouis de Limay, *J. B. Perronneau, sa vie et son oeuvre,* 1923.

Valcanover 1960
F. Valcanover, *Tutta la Pittura di Tiziano,* 2 vols., Milan 1960.

Valynseele 1954
J. Valynseele, *Le Sang des Bonapartes,* Paris 1954.

Venturi 1901-40
A. Venturi, *Storia dell'Arte Italiana,* 11 vols. in 25 parts, Milan 1901-40.

Venturi 1908
A. Venturi, 'Le opere de'pittori ferraresi del'400 secondo il catalogo di Bernardo Berenson', *L'Arte,* 1908, pp. 419-32.

Venturi 1927
A. Venturi, *Studi dal vero attraverso le raccolte artistiche d'europa,* Milan 1927.

Venturi 1931
A. Venturi, *Portrait of a Musician* under 'Lorenzo Costa' in *Enciclopedia Italiana,* vol. 11, pp. 590-91.

Voss 1907
H. Voss, *Der Ursprung des Donaustiles ein stück entwickelungsgeschichte Deutscher Malerei,* Leipzig 1907.

Voss 1925
H. Voss, 'Wolfgang Huber' in Thieme and Becker 1907-50, vol. 18, pp. 21-22.

de Vries 1977
L. de Vries, *Jan Steen, 'de kluchtschilder',* Dissertation, Groningen 1977.

Waagen 1854-57
G. F. Waagen, *Art Treasures in Great Britain,* 3 vols. and supplement, translated by Lady Eastlake, London 1854-57.

Wackernagel 1981
M. Wackernagel, *The World of the Florentine Renaissance Artist,* Princeton, 1981 (original ed. Leipzig 1938).

Walford 1991
E. J. Walford, *Jacob van Ruisdael,* New Haven and London 1991.

Walpole 1937
H. Walpole, *Anecdotes of Painting in England,* ed. Hilles and Daghlian, Yale 1937.

Waterhouse 1941
E. K. Waterhouse, *Reynolds,* London 1941.

Waterhouse 1958
E. K. Waterhouse, *Gainsborough,* London 1958.

Watson 1960
F. J. B. Watson, 'The Collections of Sir Alfred Beit: 1', *Connoisseur,* vol. 145, May 1960, pp. 156-63.

Webster 1979
M. Webster, *Hogarth,* London 1979.

Webster 1984
M. Webster, 'Wheatley's Lord and Lady Antrim', *Irish Arts Review,* vol. 1, no. 1, Spring 1984, pp. 42-45.

Webster 1989
M. Webster, 'From an Exotic Home, Hogarth's Portrait of the Mackinen Children', *Country Life,* 28 September 1989.

Weinberger 1930
M. Weinberger, *Wolfgang Huber,* Leipzig 1930.

Weisberg 1979
G. P. Weisberg, *Chardin and the Still-life Tradition in France,* Cleveland Museum of Art 1979.

Weitzmann 1961
K. Weitzmann, 'The Origin of the Threnos' in *De Artibus Opuscula XL. Essays in Honor of Erwin Panofsky,* ed. M. Meiss, vol. 1, New York University Press 1961, pp. 476-90.

Welcker 1933 and 1979
C. J. Welcker, *Hendrick Avercamp, 1585-1634, bijgenaamd 'de Stomme van Campen' en Barent Avercamp, 1612-1679, 'Schilders tot Campen',* with revised catalogue by D. J. Hensbroek-van der Poel, Doornspijk 1979 (original ed. 1933).

van Westrheene 1856
T. van Westrheene, *Jan Steen: Étude sur l'art en Hollande,* The Hague 1856.

Wethey 1969
H. E. Wethey, *Titian, vol. 2, The Religious Paintings,* London 1969.

Wethey 1972
H. E. Wethey, 'Titian's "Ecce Homo" and "Mater Dolorosa"', *Actes du xxiie. Congrès International d'Histoire et de l'Art,* 2 vols., Budapest 1969 (published 1972).

Weyerman 1726-69
J. C. Weyerman, *De Levens-beschryvingen der Nederlandsche konst-schilders en konst-schulderessen,* 4 vols., The Hague 1726-69.

Whistler 1985
C. Whistler, 'A Modello for Tiepolo's final Commission', *Apollo,* vol. 121, March 1985, pp. 172-73.

Whistler 1987
C. Whistler, review of Wynne 1986, *Irish Arts Review,* vol. 4, no. 1, Spring 1987, pp. 66-68.

White 1968
J. White, *The National Gallery of Ireland,* Dublin 1968.

Whitley 1928
W. T. Whitley, *Artists and their Friends in England 1700-1799,* 2 vols., London 1928.

Wiegand 1971
W. Wiegand, *Ruisdael-Studien: Ein Versuch zür Ikonologie der Landschaftsmalerei,* Dissertation, Hamburg 1971.

Wild 1980
D. Wild, *Nicolas Poussin,* Zurich 1980.

Wildenstein 1933, 1963 and 1969
G. Wildenstein, *J. B. S. Chardin,* Paris 1933; 2nd ed. Zurich 1963; revised and enlarged ed. by D. Wildenstein, Oxford, Glasgow and Zurich 1969.

Wildenstein 1955
G. Wildenstein, 'Les Gravures de Poussin au xviie siècle', *Gazette des Beaux-Arts,* Sept-Dec 1955, pp. 81-362 (actually published 1958).

Wildenstein 1973
D. and G. Wildenstein, *Documents complémentaires au catalogue de l'oeuvre de Louis David,* Paris 1973.

Wind 1987
B. Wind, *Velázquez's Bodegones,* Fairfax 1987.

Wine 1992
H. Wine and O. Koester, *Fransk Guldalder. Poussin og Claude og maleriet i det 17. århundredes Frankrig,* Exhibition catalogue, Statens Museum for Kunst, Copenhagen 1992.

Winternitz 1979
E. Winternitz, *Musical Instruments and their Symbolism in Western Art,* New Haven and London 1979.

Winzinger 1979
F. Winzinger, *Wolf Huber. Das Gesamtwerk,* 2 vols., Munich and Zurich 1979.

Wittkower 1973
R. Wittkower, *Art and Architecture in Italy, 1600-1750,* 3rd ed., Harmondsworth 1973.

Woodall 1935
M. Woodall, 'A Note on Gainsborough and Ruisdael', *Burlington Magazine,* vol. 66, January 1935, pp. 40-45.

Woodall 1939
M. Woodall, *Gainsborough's Landscape Drawings,* London 1939.

Woodall 1949
M. Woodall, *Thomas Gainsborough: His Life and Work,* London 1949.

Woodall 1962
M. Woodall, review of 'Gainsborough Landscapes at Nottingham University', *Burlington Magazine,* vol. 104, December 1962, pp. 561-62.

Wright 1983
C. Wright, *Dutch Landscape Painting,* Exhibition catalogue, Laing Art Gallery, Newcastle-upon-Tyne, 1983.

Wright 1985
C. Wright, *Poussin Paintings: a catalogue raisonné,* London 1985.

Wynne 1974
M. Wynne, 'The Milltowns as Patrons. Particularly concerning the picture-collecting of the first two Earls', *Apollo,* Vol. 99, February 1974, pp. 104-11.

Wynne 1986
M. Wynne, *Later Italian Paintings in the National Gallery of Ireland,* Dublin 1986.

Zapater y Gómez 1924
F. Zapater y Gómez, *Colección de cuatriocientas cuarenta y nueve reproducciones de cuadros, dibujos y aguafuertes de Don Francisco de Goya precedido de un epistolario...,* Madrid 1860; reprinted Madrid 1924.

Zeri 1974
F. Zeri, 'Major and Minor Italian Artists at Dublin', *Apollo,* vol. 99, February 1974, pp. 88-103.

LIST OF EXHIBITIONS

1739 Paris
Salon, Paris.

1774 London
Royal Academy annual exhibition, London.

1778 Rome
Palazzo Mancini, Rome.

1781 Paris
Salon, Paris.

1793 London
'The Orleans Gallery', The Great Rooms (formerly Royal Academy), Pall Mall, London.

1814 London
British Institution, London.

1815 London
British Institution, London.

1818 London
British Institution, London.

1821 London
British Institution, London.

1828 London
British Institution, London.

1832 London
British Institution, London.

1837 London
British Institution, London.

1847 Dublin
Royal Irish Art Union Exhibition, Dublin.

1857 Manchester
Art Treasures, Manchester.

1861 London
British Institution, London.

1862 London
British Institution, London.

1864 London
British Institution, London.

1865 London
British Institution, London.

1867a London
British Institution, London.

1867b London
National Portraits, South Kensington, London.

1868 Leeds
National Exhibition of Works of Art, Leeds.

1871 London
Winter Exhibition, Royal Academy, London.

1882 London
Works of the Old Masters, Royal Academy, London.

1882 Worcester
Worcestershire Exhibition, Worcester.

1883 Edinburgh
Loan Exhibition of Works by Old Masters and Scottish National Portraits, Edinburgh.

1883 London
Old Masters, Royal Academy, London.

1884 London
Exhibition of Works by the Old Masters, Royal Academy, London.

1885 London
Old Masters Exhibition, Royal Academy, London.

1894 Utrecht
Ould schilderkunst, Utrecht.

1900 London
Pictures by Dutch Masters, Burlington Fine Arts Club, London.

1902 London
Winter Exhibition, Royal Academy, London.

1906 London
Exhibition of Early German Art, Burlington Fine Arts Club, London.

1907 London
Pictures, decorative furniture etc., Burlington Fine Arts Club, London.

1909 London
Jan Steen, Dowdeswell Galleries, London.

1911 London
Exhibition of Old Masters, Grafton Galleries, London.

1911 London
Venetian Painting of the Eighteenth Century, Burlington Fine Arts Club, London.

1913-14 London
Spanish Old Masters, Grafton Galleries, London.

1916 Dublin
Royal Irish Institution 3rd Exhibition, Dublin.

1918 Dublin
Pictures by Old Masters given and bequeathed to the National Gallery of Ireland by the late Sir Hugh Lane, National Gallery of Ireland.

1918 London
18th Century French School, Burlington Fine Arts Club, London.

1920-21 London
Exhibition of Spanish Paintings, Royal Academy, London.

1925 Paris
Le Paysage Français de Poussin à Corot, Petit Palais, Paris.

1926 Leiden
Jan Steen, Leiden.

1929 London
Dutch Art 1450-1900, Royal Academy, London.

1930 London
Exhibition of Italian Art 1200-1900, Royal Academy, London.

1932 London
Exhibition of French Art 1200-1900, Royal Academy, London.

1932 Manchester
French Art Exhibition, City Art Gallery, Manchester.

1934 London
British Art c.1000-1860, Royal Academy, London.

1934 Manchester
British Art, City Art Gallery, Manchester.

1934 Paris
Le Nain, Petit Palais, Paris.

1935 Brussels
Cinq Siècles d'Art, Exposition Universelle, Brussels.

1936 Amsterdam
Twee Eeuwen Engelsche Kunst, Stedelijk Museum, Amsterdam.

1937 Paris
Chefs d'oeuvre de l'art français, Palais National des Arts, Paris.

1938 Paris
La Peinture Anglaise XVIIIe et XIX Siècles, Louvre, Paris.

1945 Nottingham
British Council Exhibition, Nottingham.

1947
An Exhibition of Spanish Paintings, The Arts Council, National Gallery, London.

1948 Rotterdam
Cornelis Troost en zijn tijd, Museum Boymans van Beuningen, Rotterdam.

1949 Florence
Lorenzo il Magnifico e le Arti, Palazzo Strozzi, Florence.

1949-50 Capetown
Old Master Paintings from the Beit Collection, National Gallery of South Africa, Capetown.

1950-51 London
Holbein and other Masters, Royal Academy of Arts, London.

1951 London
William Hogarth 1697-1764, Tate Gallery, London (British Council).

1951 Milan
Mostra del Caravaggio e dei Caravaggeschi, Palazzo Reale, Milan.

1952 Amsterdam
Drie Eeuwen Portret in Nederland, Rijksmuseum, Amsterdam.

1952 Capetown
17th Century Dutch Paintings, National Art Museum, Capetown.

1952-53 London
Dutch Pictures 1450-1750, Royal Academy, London.

1954-55 London
European Masters of the 18th Century, Royal Academy, London.

1955 Birmingham
Italian Art from the Thirteenth to the Seventeenth Century, City of Birmingham Museum and Art Gallery.

1955 Bordeaux
L'Age d'or espagnol, La Peinture en Espagne et en France autour du caravagisme, Bordeaux.

1956-57 Rome
Il Seicento Europeo, Palazzo del Espozizione, Rome.

1957 Dublin
Exhibition of Paintings from Irish Collections, Municipal Gallery of Art, Dublin.

1957 Manchester
Art Treasures Centenary Exhibition, City Art Gallery, Manchester.

1958 Dagenham
Georgian Essex (1714-1837), Valence House, Dagenham.

1958-59 The Hague
Jan Steen, Mauritshuis, The Hague.

1959 Venice
La Pittura del Seicento, Ca Pesaro, Venice.

1960 Coventry
Loan Exhibition, Herbert Art Gallery and Museum, Coventry.

1960a Paris
Louis XIV, Musée des Arts Decoratifs, Paris.

1960b Paris
Exposition Nicolas Poussin, Musée du Louvre, Paris.

1960-61 Madrid
Velázquez y lo Velazqueno, Cason del Buen Retiro, Madrid.

1961 Mantua
Andrea Mantegna, Palazzo Ducale, Mantua.

1962 Bologna
L'ideale classico del Seicento in Italia, Palazzo del Archiginnasio, Bologna.

1962 Nottingham
Landscapes by Thomas Gainsborough, Nottingham University.

1963-64 London
Goya and his Times, Royal Academy, London.

1964 London
The Art of Claude Lorrain, Hayward Gallery, London.

1964 Newcastle-upon-Tyne
The Art of Claude Lorrain, Newcastle-upon-Tyne.

1965 Jerusalem
Old Masters and the Bible, Israel Museum, Jerusalem.

1965 Kenwood
The Conversation Piece in Georgian England, Iveagh Bequest, Kenwood, London.

1965 Linz
Die Kunst der Donauschule 1490-1540, Stift St. Florian, Linz, Austria.

1966 Vienna
Die Kunst der Grafik, III, Renaissance in Italien, 16 Jahrhundert, Albertina, Vienna.

1966-67 San Francisco etc.
The Age of Rembrandt, Palace of the Legion of Honor, San Francisco; Toledo Museum of Art, Toledo, Ohio; Museum of Fine Arts, Boston.

1967 Kenwood
The Origins of Landscape Painting in England, Iveagh Bequest, Kenwood, London.

1967 London
Bi-centenary Exhibition, Christie's, London.

1968 London
France in the Eighteenth Century, Royal Academy, London.

1969 Bordeaux
L'Art et la Musique, Galerie des Beaux Arts, Bordeaux.

1970-71 The Hague and London
Shock of Recognition: the Landscape of English Romanticism and the Dutch Seventeenth-Century School, Mauritshuis, The Hague; Tate Gallery, London.

1971-72 Minneapolis etc.
Dutch Masterpieces from the eighteenth century, Institute of Arts, Minneapolis; Museum of Art, Toledo; Museum of Art, Philadelphia.

1972 London
Paintings and Sculptures 1770-1830, Heim Gallery, London.

1974-75 Paris etc.
De David à Delacroix, la peinture française de 1774 à 1830, Grand Palais, Paris; Detroit Museum of Art, Detroit; Metropolitan Museum of Art, New York.

1975 London
Master Paintings: Recent Acquisitions, Thos. Agnew and Son, London.

1975 Tokyo
English portraits from Francis Bacon the philosopher to Francis Bacon the painter, National Museum of Western Art, Tokyo.

1977 Bordeaux
La Peinture Britannique de Gainsborough à Bacon, Musée des Beaux Arts, Bordeaux.

1977-78 Rome and Düsseldorf
Nicolas Poussin (1594-1665), Villa Medici, Rome; Stadtische Kunsthalle, Düsseldorf.

1978 London
Giovanni Battista Moroni, 400th Anniversary Exhibition, National Gallery, London.

1979 London
Venetian Seventeenth-Century Painting, National Gallery, London.

1979-80 Stockholm
1700-tal, Konst och kultur under Rokokon, Nationalmuseum Stockholm.

1980-81 London
Thomas Gainsborough, Tate Gallery, London.

1981 Dublin
Recent Acquisitions 1980-1981, National Gallery of Ireland, Dublin.

1981a London
El Greco to Goya, National Gallery, London.

1981b London
Second Sight. Mantegna: Samson and Delilah. Degas: Beach Scene, National Gallery, London.

1981 Paris
Gainsborough, Grand Palais, Paris.

1981-82 Rome
David e Roma, Villa Medici, Rome.

1981-82 The Hague and Harvard
Jacob van Ruisdael, Mauritshuis, The Hague; Fogg Art Museum, Harvard University.

1982 Amsterdam and Zwolle
Hendrick Averkamp, 1585-1634. Barent Averkamp, 1612-1679: Frozen Silence, Watermann Gallery Amsterdam; Provinciaal Overijssels Museum, Zwolle.

1982 Dublin
Acquisitions 1981-1982, National Gallery of Ireland, Dublin.

1982 Kenwood
Pompeo Batoni and his British Patrons, Iveagh Bequest, Kenwood, London.

1983 Amsterdam and Groningen
Rembrandt: the Impact of a Genius, Waterman Gallery; Groningen Museum.

1983 Munich
Erlauterungen zu den ausgestellten Gemälden, Alte Pinakothek, Munich.

1983-84 London
The Genius of Venice, Royal Academy, London.

1984 Dublin
Acquisitions 1982-1983, National Gallery of Ireland, Dublin.

1984 Philadelphia etc.
Masters of 17th-Century Dutch Genre Painting, Philadelphia Museum of Art; Gemäldegalerie, Berlin; Royal Academy, London.

1985 Dublin
Le Classicisme Français: Masterpieces of seventeenth century painting, National Gallery of Ireland, Dublin.

1985 London
Masterpieces from the National Gallery of Ireland, National Gallery, London.

1985 Paris
Reynolds, Grand Palais, Paris.

1985-86 London
Reynolds, Royal Academy, London.

1986 Genoa
Il Giardino di Flora, Loggia della Mercanzia, Genoa.

1986 Paris
De Rembrandt à Vermeer: Les peintres hollandais au Mauritshuis de La Haye, Grand Palais, Paris.

1987 Amsterdam, etc.
Masters of 17th-Century Dutch Landscape Painting, Rijksmuseum, Amsterdam; Museum of Fine Arts, Boston; Philadelphia Museum of Art.

1987 Santa Ana, California etc.
Dutch Paintings of the Golden Age from the Collection of the National Gallery of Ireland, Charles W. Bowers Memorial Museum, Santa Ana, California; Midland Arts Council, Midland, Michigan; Mint Museum, Charlotte, North Carolina; Center for the Fine Arts, Miami, Florida; IBM Gallery of Science and Art, New York.

1988 Dublin
Acquisitions 1986-1988, National Gallery of Ireland, Dublin.

1989 Venice
William Hogarth: Dipinti disegni incisioni, Fondazione Giorgio Cini, Venice.

1989-90 Paris
Jacques-Louis David, 1748-1825, Grand Palais, Paris.

1990 Madrid
Velázquez, Museo del Prado, Madrid.

1990 Verona
Bernardo Bellotto, Verona e le città europee, Museo di Castelvecchio, Verona.

1990-91 Paris
Vouet, Grand Palais, Paris.

1991 Utrecht and Braunschweig
Jan Davidsz de Heem en zijn kring / Jan Davidsz de Heem und sein Kreis, Centraal Museum, Utrecht; Herzog Anton Ulrich-Museum, Braunschweig.

1992 Dublin
Caravaggio and his followers in the National Gallery of Ireland, National Gallery of Ireland, Dublin.

1992 London
Andrea Mantegna, Royal Academy, London; Metropolitan Museum of Art, New York.

INDEX OF ARTISTS